CAMBRIDGE
through student eyes

Contents

CAMBRIDGE
through student eyes

Edited, designed and produced by: Nicholas Kind
Publisher: Rebecca Thompson
University Town section written by: Mark Weatherall
Restaurant reviewers: Victor Chua, Helen Cleary, Mike Crabtree, Ron Dimant, Nicholas Joicey, Johan Khoo, Tristan Marshall, Steven Mathieson, Paul Moxon, Huy Nyguen, Diana, Miranda and Penelope Tapp, Abigail Thomas, Rebecca Thompson

Photographs: Paul Coghlan, Mike Crabtree, Jon Dick, David Jeffrey, Lizzie Judson, Johan Khoo, Nicholas Kind, R Meadows, Simon Moore, Joel Price, Matthew Smith

Thanks to: Kate Bell, Alan Hawkins, Emma Perring

Published by Varsity Publications Ltd
11-12 Trumpington Street, Cambridge CB2 1QA

ISBN 0 902240 13 7

First published 1991
Revised edition 1993

Typeset in-house in Goudy and Caslon 540 by Varsity

Photo-set by: Type & Style, 14-16 Dorland House, Regent Street, London SW1Y 4PH

Printed and bound by: Ennisfield Print and Design, Telfords Yard, 6-8 The Highway, Wapping London E1 9BQ

Cover illustration of the Bridge of Sighs and 'University Life' lino cut by: Ho Wuon Gean, St John's College, Cambridge

THE UNIVERSITY CITY

The University Town

Before there was Gown, there was Town. There has been a settlement of sorts on the banks of the river since Roman times. The bridge, from which the town takes its name, was built by the Saxons in the 7th century (or 8th, or maybe 9th, depending on who you believe).

It was always an important place. After the Romans left, the river (known to the Saxons as the Granta, and today as the Cam) divided the kingdom of the Mercians from that of the East Angles. The Saxons called the town Grantanbrycge, the Normans called it Grantebrigge, Chaucer called it Cantebrigge.

The Backs

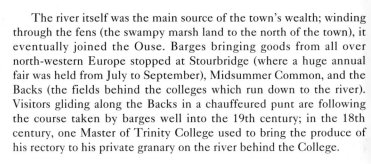
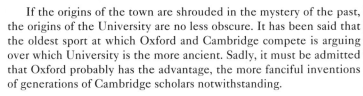

The river itself was the main source of the town's wealth; winding through the fens (the swampy marsh land to the north of the town), it eventually joined the Ouse. Barges bringing goods from all over north-western Europe stopped at Stourbridge (where a huge annual fair was held from July to September), Midsummer Common, and the Backs (the fields behind the colleges which run down to the river). Visitors gliding along the Backs in a chauffeured punt are following the course taken by barges well into the 19th century; in the 18th century, one Master of Trinity College used to bring the produce of his rectory to his private granary on the river behind the College.

If the origins of the town are shrouded in the mystery of the past, the origins of the University are no less obscure. It has been said that the oldest sport at which Oxford and Cambridge compete is arguing over which University is the more ancient. Sadly, it must be admitted that Oxford probably has the advantage, the more fanciful inventions of generations of Cambridge scholars notwithstanding.

It is well documented that, in 1209, following the killing of an Oxford student by some townsmen, the scholars went on strike. This was a serious business; in mediaeval times, the presence of a band of scholars in a town meant lucrative trade. The resulting diaspora of Oxford academics settled in several towns, but only in Cambridge did the settlement become permanent.

This immediately led to trouble. The scholars did not just bring their learning with them, but also knives, sticks and a bad attitude. Though the University was as yet unofficial, it assumed all the traditional rights of such a body. Conflicts grew increasingly fractious—one Chancellor even excommunicated the Mayor—and the University's hand was strengthened when in 1318, at the urging of Edward II, it was officially recognised by Pope John XXII.

Relations with townsfolk reached their lowest ebb in 1381, when a mob led by the mayor and burgesses sacked most of the University buildings, and burnt all the documents they could lay their hands on with a cry of "Away with the skill of the Clerks!" Retribution for these acts was swift, and came in the form of the King granting the University control over many aspects of the life of the town, including the pricing of bread, wine and ale, the checking of weights and measures, and the licensing of entertainments, rights which the University retained until the 19th century.

Most of the colleges, those communities which distinguish Oxford and Cambridge from most other universities, were founded in three waves. The first wave, founded from 1284 to 1352, were simply student halls of residence; St Peter's (or Peterhouse) was the first, followed by Michael House and King's Hall (both of which became parts of Trinity College), Clare Hall, Pembroke Hall, Gonville Hall, Trinity Hall and Bene't Hall (now Corpus Christi College). Several of these still survive, though only Peterhouse and Trinity Hall retain their original names; the rest have become known as colleges, or have been refounded under different designations.

*St John's College
Old Bridge*

The second wave occurred in the Tudor age, from 1441 (when King's College was founded) to 1594 (Sidney Sussex). Ironically, many of these colleges (Queens', Trinity, St John's, Magdalene and Jesus) were built of red brick. The third wave has occurred over the last hundred years or so, and, mirroring the extensive changes which occurred in the University in the 19th century, includes the foundation of colleges for women and research students.

Like all mediaeval universities, Cambridge was home to scholars in all four of the great faculties of theology, medicine, law and the arts. Students wandered from university to university in search of the greatest teachers of the day; Cambridge was home to students from all over Europe. The Dutch scholar Erasmus, perhaps the greatest scholar of the Renaissance, taught at Queens' College between 1510 and 1513. He didn't enjoy it much, complaining incessantly about the cost of living in Cambridge (*plus ça change*), but he did like the women of the town, whom he called "divinely pretty, soft, pleasant, gentle, and charming as the Muses".

The conflicts that engulfed England over the next two hundred years were mirrored in Cambridge. During the 16th century, Cambridge became a hotbed of Protestantism, many of her alumni being burnt at the stake for their faith in the 1530s and 1540s. Clashes between Papists and Protestants were a regular feature of University life through much of the century. One hundred years later, Cambridge was again rent in two by the Civil War; this time the division was along the by now traditional lines of Town (who supported Cromwell) and Gown (who supported the King, despite claiming Cromwell as one of its alumni). Not surprisingly, the University suffered under the Protectorate, but regained its position when Charles II was restored to the throne. This was also a period of great

A petition organised by members of the students' union executive

advancement of learning: to name but one participant in this process, Isaac Newton, discoverer of gravity, lived and worked at Trinity College.

The 18th century is commonly supposed to be the nadir of the University's history, a period when students and scholars alike did little other than drink, gamble and carouse. It is certainly true that the energies of the University were not directed towards teaching, but this was because, at no time in the University's history, have its affairs been so intimately bound up with intrigue, influence, and all the other aspects of the new party politics. By the end of the century, however, the long neglect of its academic basis had begun to affect its reputation. Samuel Taylor Coleridge, who came up to Jesus College in 1791, wrote, "In Cambridge there are sixteen Colleges that look like workhouses, and fourteen churches that look like little houses. The town is very fertile in alleys, and mud, and cats, and dogs, besides men, women, ravens, clergy, proctors, tutors, owls, and other two-legged cattle."

A traveller from 1600 would have found much of the University of 1800 very familiar. The University's primary function was to educate the minds of young men who would enter the church; the study of mathematics was considered to be the best way of achieving this. By 1900, however, everything had changed. The town expanded and, with the coming of the railway in 1845, became more cosmopolitan. The University underwent an enormous expansion, both in numbers of students and the range of subjects taught. Students no longer had to be members of the Church of England. Extra-mural examinations were instituted. Lecture courses and examinations were opened to women. The traditional faculties were supplemented by laboratories of science, both pure and applied, teachers of multifarious languages both living and dead, and diverse new philosophies. All this change came under the influence of outside competition (the University of London was founded in the 1830s), outside scrutiny (Royal Commissions in the 1850s and 1870s), and a reforming instinct from within, which one historian has called 'the revolution of the dons'.

The changes set underway in the second half of the 19th century gathered pace at the beginning of this century. Burgeoning numbers of research students found a home in the University. The reputation of the University's scientific departments—particularly the Cavendish Laboratory and the Institute of Biochemistry—grew and grew, numerous Nobel Prizes being garnered by scientists educated in, or based in Cambridge. Women were finally admitted to degrees in 1947 and, in the 1970s, the colleges began to go mixed (the last all-male bastion being breached when Magdalene went mixed in 1988). Students campaigned for a voice in the academic affairs of the University; an effective University-wide Students' Union developed in the early 1970s.

The Cavendish Laboratory site

The Seely Library, part of the Arts site on Sidgwick Avenue

It is easy to see Cambridge as a place of unchanging tradition and beauty, but this is far from the case. Today, in the early 1990s, the pace of change is as rapid as ever. New departments are being created, and old ones renovated, funded by a massive development appeal, to keep Cambridge at the forefront of the academic world. The academic centre of gravity of the University, which has shifted over the centuries from the Old Schools, and is currently split between the Science area off Downing Street and the Arts' site on Sidgwick Avenue, is set to shift yet again to West Cambridge, where green field sites are earmarked for University use. In 50 years' time, Cambridge will have changed out of all recognition, but it is the continuing ability of the University and the town to adapt to the vicissitudes of culture that have shaped the history of this University town.

The University Today

C ambridge is a 'collegiate' university. It has no campus, but rather a collection of colleges and academic departments. All students are junior members of one of the 31 colleges (six colleges are devoted to graduates, and three are for women only). Many, but not all, of the University's academics are also fellows (senior members) of one of the colleges. The college is the centre of the undergraduate's life: it provides accommodation, food, individual tuition, pastoral care, and entertainments (usually organised by the students themselves).

The departments are responsible for organising lectures and (where appropriate) practical work for undergraduates. Each department has its own library. They also contain many graduate students working for advanced degrees (doctorates or master's degrees). Most departments run seminar series and academic meetings to which a broad range of researchers contribute—from nervous PhD students giving their first ever paper, to leading figures in each field. The departments are grouped together into faculties; these bodies co-ordinate the teaching curricula, set examinations, and judge the quality of research submitted for advanced degrees.

The power of actually granting degrees rests with the University, rather than the colleges or departments. Degrees are given at a ceremony held several times a year at the Senate House, on King's Parade. The largest of these ceremonies is the General Admission to BA degrees, spread over two days at the end of June, at which nearly all the final year undergraduates (some 3,000 in all) receive their degrees; by a curious quirk of Cambridge tradition, all undergraduates receive BA (Bachelor of Arts) degrees, even if they have studied a scientific subject.

The new University Library

Behind the Senate House are the Old Schools. These buildings housed the faculties and the University Library until the early 19th century; they now contain the University's administrative centre. The University Library moved from this site in 1934 to its modern home across the river, the work of Giles Gilbert Scott. The Library is one of the country's five copyright libraries, entitled by law to a copy of any book published in this country. Whilst in practice the Library does not actually take every book, it does have an enormous collection of over 4 million volumes (many of which are very rare, or even unique), as well as extensive manuscript holdings.

A significant proportion of the books held in the University Library were published in Cambridge by the University Press. The Press dates back to 1534, when it was granted a charter by Henry VIII. The Press was once housed in the Pitt building on Trumpington St, built in 1833 with the surplus from public subscriptions for a statue of William Pitt (Prime Minister 1783-1805). Although it still maintains offices in the building, the Press has now moved most of its operations to new premises near the railway station. The church-like appearance of the Pitt building's façade led to its being dubbed "the Freshers' church", after the hoax played on generations of Cambridge freshmen who were informed that their presence was required there on the first Sunday of the academic year. Even today, one may spot the occasional bemused, begowned student outside the building on the second Sunday in October.

The current Vice-Chancellor, Professor Sir David Williams

The University is a self-governing body. The position of Chancellor is, and has been for many centuries, largely ceremonial. Real influence rests with the Vice-Chancellor, who presides over the Council of Senate, which is made up of senior fellows of the University. The Council's proposals—known as 'graces'—are debated by the University's resident fellows. A vote is held upon a matter if, when the grace is read out, one of the fellows says "non placet" ('it does not please'). The reports of the Council of Senate and the graces are printed in the *Cambridge University Reporter*, the official university journal; although the *Reporter* is not supposed to carry any controversial material, it does have an 'unofficial' section in which the often heated debates are closely reported. The Vice-Chancellorship used to be a part-time job, held for two years by one of the Heads of the Colleges; due to recent changes in the University's administrative structure, the present incumbent, Sir David Williams, is the first full-time Vice-Chancellor.

Discipline is maintained within colleges by the Dean, who has the power to fine offenders if he or she sees fits. At a University level, the officials responsible for discipline are called 'proctors'. The job of proctor is today far less onerous, and far less dangerous, than in the past. In years gone by, the proctors would patrol the city's streets, wearing gown and mortar board, accompanied by two 'bulldogs' (burly porters who could catch, and restrain, unruly students), checking that students weren't frequenting undesirable hostelries, or committing the truly heinous crime of not wearing their gown.

The Colleges

Much of the charm of central Cambridge stems from the intimate character of the college courts and the beauty of the ancient buildings. The most picturesque of the colleges are the oldest, largely to be found along the river and around the city centre. These are all within a short walk of each other, mostly along the Backs. Each college has its own distinctive character and unique history, explaining the way it is today.

Colleges are headed by a Master or Mistress, except for King's (a Provost), Queens', New Hall, Wolfson and Clare Hall (Presidents), Newnham (a Principal) and Robinson (a Warden). Other senior members of college are usually called Fellows. All are elected largely on the basis of their academic achievements. Most have heavy teaching and administrative duties, but all regard their own research as equally important. The number of students in each college varies from fewer than 100 to nearly 1000, of which usually two thirds or more are undergraduates. Most colleges house all their undergraduates, and students may find themselves living in rooms which are centuries old.

Visitors should bear in mind that the colleges are places where people live and work. For this reason, parts of many of the colleges remain closed to the public at all times, and many are closed altogether during the examinations period in May and June. In addition, groups of ten or more people wishing to tour the colleges must be accompanied by a bluebadged Cambridge guide. Details are available from the Tourist Information Centre.

The Ancient Colleges

Peterhouse

Peterhouse (never 'Peterhouse College'), on Trumpington St, is small, having around 300 students. It is the oldest college, being founded in 1284 by Hugh de Balsham, Bishop of Ely. The first Master and fourteen Fellows were left 300 marks by the founder and built the Hall, the only original building to survive. It contains wonderful examples of stained glass and tiling by William Morris dating from its restoration in the 1870s. The Library and Chapel were added in 1628 during the Mastership of Matthew Wren, uncle of the great architect Sir Christopher Wren. Peterhouse was the first college to have electricity, the work of Lord Kelvin, a member of the college. Other members have included the poet Thomas Gray, the scientist Henry Cavendish, Charles Babbage, inventor of the first mechanical computer, and Sir Frank Whittle, inventor of the jet engine. Today, Peterhouse has a strong reputation for traditionalism.

Opposite Peterhouse stands **Pembroke College**, founded in 1347. Its much-restored gatehouse is the most notable survival from the time of its foundress, Marie de St Pol de Valence, Countess of Pembroke. Her original court, now Old Court, was partly demolished in the 19th century, as was the Hall, which was rebuilt by Alfred Waterhouse in 1875. The Chapel was the first building to be completed by Sir Christopher Wren, and was the first truly Classical building in Cambridge. It replaced the original chapel, which was used until the last century as a library. Hitcham's building and cloister were added at about the same time, and the rest of the college is modern. Pembroke men have included William Pitt the younger and the poet Edmund Spenser. Fellow poet Thomas Gray came to Pembroke to escape practical jokes being played on him at Peterhouse. The Poet Laureate, Ted Hughes, and the inventor of the Dolby System, Ray Dolby, were at Pembroke more recently.

At the near end of King's Parade is **Corpus Christi College**. Established in 1352, it is unique among the colleges of Oxford and Cambridge in being founded by townsfolk. Old Court, which is the best surviving example of an early mediaeval college court, is situated right in the centre of the ancient town. The rest of the college was built in 1823 by William Wilkins, architect both of Downing and of much of King's. Corpus' greatest treasure is its library, which includes the 6th century Canterbury Gospel, Anglo-Saxon manuscripts and mediaeval books presented by Archbishop Parker in 1575. The Elizabethan playwright and rival to Shakespeare, Christopher Marlowe, graduated from Corpus in 1587; a portrait believed to be his hangs in the Hall. Other alumni include the writers John Cowper Powys and Christopher Isherwood.

Old Court,
Corpus Christi College

Further up King's Parade is another of the smaller colleges, **St Catharine's College** (known to undergraduates as 'Catz'). It was founded by the third Provost of neighbouring King's, Robert Woodlark, in 1473. Most of the college dates from a comprehensive rebuilding started in 1673 and completed in 1775. The original entrance was in Queens' Lane, but the fourth side of the court, on Trumpington St, was never built. Today Catz is strong on engineering students, but past members have included Dr John Addenbrooke, and William Wotton, who entered in 1675 aged nine but already fluent in Latin, Greek and Hebrew.

Across Queens' Lane is **Queens' College**. Originally founded in 1446 as St Bernard's College, it was refounded in 1448 by Queen Margaret of Anjou, wife of Henry VII, founder of King's. When Henry was deposed, his successor's wife, Queen Elizabeth Woodville, carried on the work, and the college considers itself founded by both women (hence the placing of the apostrophe in its name after the 's'). Old Court, finished in 1449, has survived virtually unaltered, although the Hall was heavily restored in the 19th century. Nearby Cloister Court is dominated by the beautiful half-

Cloister Court, Queens' College

timbered Tudor Long Gallery of the President's Lodge. The cloisters make a remarkably atmospheric setting for student productions of Shakespeare during the summer. Queens' straddles the Backs, the world-famous river frontage of the colleges, and its two halves are linked by the Mathematical Bridge, rumoured originally to have been constructed entirely without nails, to a design by Newton. This, however, is a myth—Newton died 22 years before the bridge was built. The scholar Erasmus taught Greek at Queens' in 1510-14, and a tower in Pump Court bears his name. Modern famous names include the comedian and actor Stephen Fry.

King's College, neighbour to both Queens' and Catz, provides the two classic views of Cambridge. Approached from the Backs, the Chapel and James Gibbs' Fellows' building (1724) come first into sight. On King's Parade, the Chapel and William Wilkins' gatehouse and screen dominate. King's Chapel is without doubt the most magnificent building in Cambridge. Started in 1446, five years after the College's foundation, work dragged on through five reigns and a civil war (the Wars of the Roses) before completion in 1515. Henry VI originally envisaged a huge college, with an arcaded front court, giant bell tower and a cloistered court on the Backs. To this end, he bought and razed a large part of the mediaeval city centre. His subsequent overthrow meant that the site remained empty for three hundred years, to the chagrin of the townsfolk, and the college was housed in what is now the Old Schools. The front court was only completed in the 1830s, and most of the college is more modern still. King's College Choir is the best in Cambridge, recording and broadcasting regularly. King's is not dominated by its Chapel, however. Once the home of literary men Rupert Brooke, E M Forster and Salman Rushdie, and the great economist J M Keynes (later College Bursar), the college now has a reputation for political radicalism among students and Fellows.

Clare College

Looking onto King's back lawn are the delightful buildings of **Clare College**. The second oldest college, Clare was founded in 1326 by the University as an equivalent to Oxford's University College, but poverty led to its refounding by Lady Elizabeth de Clare in 1338. Many of the original buildings burned down in 1521, and today's Clare was built, with many interruptions including the English Civil War, between 1638 and 1719. The Chapel, dating from 1760, has a dramatic octagonal ante-chapel, unique in Cambridge. Clare Bridge, built by the Cambridge builder Robert Grumbold in 1638, is the oldest of the college bridges. An old trick is to ask visitors to count the balls on it: the strange but correct answer is thirteen and four fifths, as a segment has been shaved off one of them. The Fellows' Garden is noted for its beauty. Old Court is pretty but cramped, and in 1922 work began across the river on Memorial Court (designed by Sir Giles Gilbert Scott), in memory of college members killed in World War I. The Protestant reformer and martyr Hugh Latimer was a Fellow during the 16th century.

A classic view; King's College from the Backs

Trinity College Great Court

Walking into Trinity Lane, one comes to the 'Lawyers' College', **Trinity Hall**, affectionately known as 'Tit Hall'. Founded in 1350 by Bishop Bateman of Norwich, it was intended to provide a new body of priests and lawyers following the ravages of the Black Death. The main court, dating from the 14th century, was refaced in the 18th century and largely rebuilt after a fire in 1852. The loveliest building is the Elizabethan Library, which contains Jacobean bookcases complete with the original books, chained to prevent theft. The stunning herbaceous borders by the Library were described by the novelist Henry James as "the prettiest corner of the world". The Chapel, Cambridge's smallest, dates from 1352, and has stained glass commemorating Robert Runcie, Dean from 1956-60 and later Archbishop of Canterbury. Apart from the army of eminent judges and lawyers, Tit Hall has produced Viscount Fitzwilliam, founder of the Fitzwilliam Museum, and the writers Bulwer-Lytton, Ronald Firbank and J B Priestley.

Gargoyle, Gonville and Caius College

Looming at the end of King's Parade is the Victorian tower of **Gonville and Caius College**. Usually known as 'Caius' (pronounced 'keys'), it was founded in 1348 as Gonville Hall by Edmund Gonville. Gonville Court, built between 1441 and 1490, is all that survives. The college was refounded in 1557 by Dr John Caius, a former student and physician to three monarchs, after much of its land had been seized by Henry VIII for his new college, Trinity. Caius greatly increased the college's endowments, and added a new court, which bears his name. He also erected the three famous gates, of Humility, Virtue and Honour, symbolising his ideal of a student's career. Modern Caius undergraduates still pass through the gate of Honour on their way to the Senate House on Degree Day. The huge buildings on Trinity St and Tree Court, which were completed in 1870, are the work of Alfred Waterhouse (who also built at Pembroke), and have been described as "the most despised buildings in Cambridge". A large college, and one of the richest, Caius has traditionally been strong on medicine, with members such as the physiologist William Harvey, who discovered the circulation of the blood.

Big though Caius may be, it is dwarfed by Cambridge's largest college, **Trinity College**. Founded by Henry VIII five weeks before his death in 1547, Trinity was amalgamated from two smaller colleges, King's Hall and Michaelhouse. The Great Court is the largest college court in either Cambridge or Oxford, and is the work of Thomas Neville, Master from 1593 and a favourite of Elizabeth I. The Court has over two acres of lawns and paths, and is the original scene of the traditional 'Great Court Run'—a race around the court while the clock strikes twelve—featured in the film *Chariots of Fire* (although the scene was filmed at Eton). The Elizabethan Fountain was once the college's main water supply. Neville not only created Great Court, but also his own, smaller court, beyond the Hall (the largest hall in Cambridge). This cloistered court, erected in 1612,

The Pepys Library, Magdalene College

was originally open to the river, but is now closed by Sir Christopher Wren's Library. Completed in 1695, it is one of Cambridge's most beautiful classical buildings. Nearby is William Wilkins' 19th century New Court, and on Trinity Lane the delightful 17th century Bishop's Hostel. Trinity's buildings also include Whewell's Court, opposite the Great Gate, and other buildings nearby: one pleasant modern development incorporates what was the old Blue Boar Hotel, the last of the old central Cambridge hotels. Trinity boasts over a score of Nobel Prize winners, and its alumni include Sir Isaac Newton, whose rooms were near the Great Gate, Sir Francis Bacon, the philosopher Bertrand Russell, the poets Dryden, Herbert and Marvell, and Prince Charles. Byron kept a pet bear while he was at Trinity. While Trinity may be famous for producing six Prime Ministers, it is best known to today's students for its size and wealth: an undergraduate myth states that it is possible to walk from Cambridge to Oxford solely upon land by either Trinity College Cambridge or Trinity College Oxford.

Crest, St John's College

A few yards up the road is **St John's College**, one of the larger colleges. The elaborate gatehouse bears the arms of the foundress, Lady Margaret Beaufort, who established the college posthumously in 1511 on the site of a 13th century hospital formerly run by the Order of St John. Her arms are supported by Yales, mythical beasts with goats' heads, antelopes' bodies and elephants' tails. The Tudor First Court was followed in 1598 by the Second Court, financed by Mary, Countess of Shrewsbury, while Third Court is mainly 17th century. The old bridge was built between 1708 and 1712 by Robert Grumbold from sketches by Sir Christopher Wren. Today it provides an excellent view of Henry Hutchinson's Bridge of Sighs, built in 1831 in imitation of its Venetian namesake to link the old college with New Court. New Court is a 19th century Gothic fairy-tale ideal of how a college should look, and is irreverently known as 'The Wedding Cake'. Hidden behind New Court is the award-winning modern Cripps Building, completed in 1967. The Chapel, built in 1863-9, is the work of Sir Gilbert Scott. Old Johnians include William Wordsworth, who described his First Court rooms in *The Prelude*, and more recently, Douglas Adams, cult author of *The Hitch-Hiker's Guide to the Galaxy*.

Just across Magdalene Bridge stands **Magdalene College** (pronounced 'Maudlin'). Founded in 1428 as Buckingham College, it originally housed only monks. The dissolution of the monasteries under Henry VIII brought the college to its knees, but it was refounded by Lord Audley of Walden in 1542. The Chapel dates from the 1480s. Samuel Pepys was a Magdalene man, and left his 3000-volume library to the college on his death in 1703. This is housed in the Pepys Building in Second Court, in its twelve original red oak bookcases. Chief among the collection's treasures is Pepys' personal coded diary (first published in 1825), which took three years to decipher. Many of the modern undergraduates are housed in courts on the other side of Magdalene St. One of these is named after A E Benson, Master and author of the words to *Land of Hope and Glory*, and another after George L Mallory, who died within feet of the summit of Mount Everest in 1924. The Magdalene of today has a conservative reputation, being the last male undergraduate college to admit women.

Magdalene is the last ancient college on the river. Further inland, by Jesus Green, stands **Jesus College**. Its spacious grounds once belonged to the Priory of St Radegund, dating from the 1130s. The priory fell into disrepute, and was refounded as a college by John Alcock, Bishop of Ely, in 1496. Alcock converted the priory's buildings to scholastic use, adding the gatehouse, which today stands at the end of a walled passage known as 'The Chimney'. Cloister Court is Tudor, but the open arches were added in 1768. Chapel Court was extended in 1928 and includes carvings by the sculptor Eric Gill. The 1960s North Court includes rooms occupied by Prince Edward when he came up in 1983; other members have included Thomas Cranmer (the Archbishop of Canterbury martyred by Queen Mary in 1556), the writer Samuel Taylor Coleridge, and the journalist Alastair Cooke. One of the college's treasures is a copy of the first Bible to be published in America. It was printed at Cambridge, Massachusetts in 1663, and translated into Algonquin by the college's John Eliot, who attempted to convert the North American Indians to Christianity. Jesus is noted for its sporting prowess, particularly on the river.

Jesus College;
'The Chimney'

In the heart of the City's shopping centre is **Sidney Sussex College**, known to undergraduates as 'Sidney Sainsbury's' as it stands opposite a branch of the supermarket chain. Sidney Sussex was the last of the older colleges to be established, being founded on the site of a former friary in 1596. It draws its name from Lady Frances Sidney, Countess of Sussex, who bequeathed £5000 towards its foundation. The hotch-potch of 16th and 17th century buildings was refaced by Sir Jeffry Wyatville in the early 19th century. Although his work is not universally admired, he created the two uniform front courts from a rather disparate group of buildings. The delightful Chapel was designed by James Essex in 1774 and extended in 1912. Although Oliver Cromwell, Lord Protector of England, was a Sidney man, the College supported the King during the English Civil War. Cromwell's body was exhumed and beheaded on Charles II's orders after the Restoration; the head eventually came into the college's possession and was buried in great secrecy in the Chapel in 1960 in the presence of the Master, the chaplain and three Fellows.

Christ's College, in St Andrew's St, was originally founded on a site near the river as God's House in 1439 by the Revd William Byngham. Displaced by Henry VI's plans to build King's, it moved in 1446. Progress was slow, and in 1505 Lady Margaret Beaufort, who also founded St John's, refounded it as Christ's College. The beautiful First Court was built at this time (but refaced in the 18th century), and the Fellows' Building was started in 1640, reputedly to a design by Inigo Jones. Further building has occurred since, most notably Sir Denys Lasdun's New Court (1966), known to undergraduates as Christ's 'Typewriter'. Christ's has been home to the poet John Milton, who was nicknamed 'the Lady of Christ's' because of his delicate appearance, and Charles Darwin, author of *The Origin of Species*.

*Front Court,
Emmanuel College*

A little way along St Andrew's St is the 18th century entrance to **Emmanuel College**, known affectionately to students as 'Emma'. Founded in 1584 by Sir Walter Mildmay, Chancellor to Elizabeth I, it occupies the site of a Dominican Priory dissolved by Henry VIII. Mildmay intended the college to be "a seed-plot of learned men", priests for the newly established Protestant Church. The college became a centre for theology in Cambridge, and many of the first Protestant settlers in New England were from Emmanuel; among these was John Harvard, founder of Harvard University. The original monastic buildings were adapted by the founder, who, to emphasize the changes in religious thinking, made the old priory church into a dining-hall and the refectory into the chapel. This chapel was never consecrated and was unconventionally aligned, and it was replaced in 1677 by a new one in First Court, designed by Sir Christopher Wren. The rest of First Court was rebuilt in the 18th century. Old Court, formerly and unimaginatively called 'Brick Building', was built in 1633. The original college court, now called New Court, was extended in the 1820s.

The Younger Colleges

For over 200 years after Sidney Sussex was founded, no new colleges were established in Cambridge. This long inactivity was broken in 1800 with the foundation of **Downing College**, on Regent St. Downing would have been started years before but for a long legal battle between the relatives of the founder, Baronet Sir George Downing, and the University. The battle left the legacy much reduced, and while work was started by William Wilkins in a neo-Classical idiom in the early 19th century, the college remained unfinished until modern times. Wilkins eschewed the mediaeval tradition for college courts, creating instead a large turfed campus, anticipating the first American campus university (at Virginia) by some years. Downing thus makes a pleasant and spacious change from the older colleges. It has a sporty reputation today.

Downing was the last college to be established for general educational purposes in the ancient tradition. All those founded since have been created to fulfil a particular educational need, usually to provide for women's education. **Girton College**, two and a half miles from the City and the first of the women's colleges, was founded in 1869. Originally located in the Hertfordshire town of Hitchin, it moved to Girton village, felt to be a safe distance from the dangers of Cambridge's menfolk, in 1873. The 50 acres of grounds are immaculate, and the buildings, the work of Sir Alfred Waterhouse in his best Tudor Gothic style, are pleasant. In 1978 the college admitted its first male students. Inevitably it is best known among undergraduates for being very, very far away from the city centre.

Newnham College, the second women's college, opened as Newnham Hall in 1875. It had been started in 1871 when Henry Sidgwick, a Fellow of Trinity, rented houses to provide lodgings for female students. The college received its Charter in 1919. Newnham's listed buildings, designed in a William and Mary style by Sir Basil Champneys, are warm and attractive and mostly date from around the turn of the century. The college's several residential halls—there are no courts—are linked by a corridor rumoured to be the longest in Europe. There is no chapel, Newnham being strictly non-denominational, but the college does include the first Cambridge college building to be designed by a woman, Elizabeth Whitworth Scott's Fawcett Building. Old Newnhamites include the poet Sylvia Plath. Newnham is still a single-sex college.

Neighbouring **Selwyn College** was established in 1882 by public subscription to "make provision for those who intend to serve as missionaries overseas and... to educate the sons of clergymen". Membership was originally restricted to baptised Christians, and charges to undergraduates were kept low to encourage poorer students. Since then, Selwyn has become very much a mainstream, midsized, mixed-sex college.

Homerton College is Cambridge's famous teacher training college, preparing students mainly for the Bachelor of Education degree (the 'BEd'). Originally based in Homerton Village, Middlesex, it moved in 1894 to its present buildings on the outskirts of Cambridge, previously home to the now-defunct Cavendish College. Homerton stopped admitting men in 1897, but became mixed once again in 1978.

Homerton College

The Modern Colleges

The extreme shortage of women's places in British Universities in the years after World War II led to the formation of an association with the sole aim of founding a third Cambridge college for women. The result was **New Hall**, opened in 1954. Originally set up as a limited company, the college

Newnham College

moved from its first home near the Backs to a larger site a little further from the city centre in 1964. The new buildings, designed by architects Chamberlin, Powell and Bon, are most notable for the towering white dining-hall dome. This was painted one night with huge black footprints by undergraduate pranksters.

Next door to New Hall is **Fitzwilliam College**. Fitzwilliam was granted a Charter in 1966, but had already existed for nearly 100 years as Fitzwilliam Hall, the organisation for University students who for various reasons were not members of colleges. Formerly based opposite the Fitzwilliam Museum (hence its name), the Hall had grown to over 400 members by 1946, making it one of the largest establishments in the University. Its older buildings are the work of Sir Denys Lasdun. 'Fitz' alumni include Singaporean leader Lee Kuan Yew and British politician and Master of Emmanuel College, Lord St John of Fawsley.

Churchill College

Churchill College is the national monument to Sir Winston Churchill. The college's Archive Centre contains a collection of his papers. Churchill was inspired by a visit to the Massachusetts Institute of Technology to address the problem of Britain's shortage of science graduates. For this reason, 70% of Churchill's students are scientists, and a third are graduates. The College received its Charter in 1960 and opened in modern buildings in 1966. The 40 acres of grounds contain some fine modern sculpture, including a large Hepworth. Churchill was the first previously all-male college to admit women, doing so in 1972.

The most recent college to be founded is **Robinson College**. It is the gift of a single benefactor, Sir David Robinson, who donated £18 million for its establishment. The college was opened by the Queen in 1981, and stands on a twelve-acre site near the University Library. Designed by Glasgow architects Gillespie, Kidd and Coia, the college is the only one to have been built with students of both sexes in mind. The Chapel, with stained glass by John Piper, is spectacularly beautiful.

The University boasts another six foundations. Mostly dating from the 19th and 20th centuries, their members comprise a mixture of graduates and mature undergraduates. **Hughes Hall, Darwin College, St Edmund's College, Wolfson College** and **Clare Hall** are all mainly for graduate students. **Lucy Cavendish College** is unique not only in Cambridge, but also in Europe in offering places exclusively for mature women students to read for any University degree, allowing them to resume their studies.

UNIVERSITY
LIFE

Passing—the 1992 Varsity Match

A year in Cambridge

As with most other British universities, the Cambridge University year starts in early October. The first week of the first term, known as the Michaelmas Term, sees not only the return of students, but also an influx of fresh faces into the colleges. First-year undergraduate students, known as 'freshers' are introduced into Cambridge life with a whirlwind week of tea-parties, jazz-nights, cocktails and pub crawls, organised by the colleges' student unions.

The freshers fair

An important part of 'Freshers' Week', as the period is known, is the annual societies fair in Cambridge's sports hall. A vivid, seething mass of banners and posters, the fair is entirely made up of stalls for societies busily recruiting new members. A society will customarily hold a 'squash'—undergraduate slang for a recruitment meeting—at which incentives will be offered to prospective members. These invariably involve free drink, and the wary squash-goer always ensures that he does not attend with his cheque book in his pocket, in case he becomes carried away and pays his subscription right away. Societies vary from the deeply serious to the entirely flippant—Student Community Action, for example, channels students into voluntary work, whilst the activities of the Penguin Equality and Natural Instincts Society apparently include 'discussing flippered fauna'.

During the festivities of Freshers' Week, the new undergraduates have to learn to settle into a hectic cycle of essays, practicals, lectures and supervisions, whilst fitting in their extra-curricular interests and time to see their new-found friends. The Michaelmas Term, being furthest away from the examinations in the summer, is a time at which some students try out new interests. Many try rowing for the first time, as most colleges have thriving Boat Clubs who are eager to press undergraduates or graduates into an eight or a four.

'Full Term', the period during which teaching goes on, lasts only eight weeks, a comparatively short time compared to many other British universities. However, students are expected to do considerable amounts of reading during their vacations. The Michaelmas Term proper ends towards the beginning of December, and is heralded by a series of seasonal events. At the ADC Theatre, home of Cambridge student drama, the annual pantomime is produced by the Cambridge Footlights Club. Dating back to the last century, 'Footlights' is a society specialising in comedy, and has produced comedians such as Stephen Fry, David Frost and John Cleese. Their pantomime is usually not the family show traditional in other British theatres.

Christmas is celebrated early at the end of the term. Colleges hold Christmas dinners and mulled wine and mince pies parties before most decorations have gone up. These are often boisterous occasions—one college's dinner regularly sees the students standing on the tables and singing Christmas carols after their meal.

In the week after term has ended, the annual Varsity Rugby Match is held at Twickenham. Guaranteed a world-wide audience, the annual fixture against Oxford continues to produce world-class players who progress to the international scene. It was only a few years ago that Gavin Hastings and Rob Andrew, who have captained Scotland and England respectively, wore the light blue of Cambridge University.

Some students remain in Cambridge after the end of term. Amongst the most important of these during the Christmas vacation are the members of King's College Chapel Choir. The service of Nine Lessons and Carols from King's, traditionally the service which is broadcast on national television and radio, always heralds a packed chapel.

The Christmas vacation is a tense time for school-leavers applying to Cambridge. Having chosen their college and course earlier in the year, they will come up for interviews in the first weeks of December. In early January, they will hear whether or not they have been successful. Some lucky applicants will receive an offer of a place dependent on the results of their 'A' levels or Highers in the summer, the English and Scottish secondary school exams taken at eighteen.

Queens' College students during the rag procession, which heralds the beginning of 'Rag Week'

Perhaps if January, February and March were not sometimes very cold, the Lent Term would not be the term in which Cambridge Rag, the student fund-raising society, decides to cheer up the city. Cambridge was the first to stage a student 'rag' with Oxford University over 100 years ago. Today, it regularly collects over £100,000 annually for a variety of local charities.

Traditional Rag events include Blind Date night, when hundreds of students are randomly paired up for the evening, and the Bed Race which originally started amongst the medical students at Addenbrooke's Hospital. These and many other activities culminate in a frenzy of sponsored fund-raising in Rag Week, towards the end of the Lent Term. Anything and everything from water-pistol 'hit squads' and 'rent-a-gnome' services (pixies who are paid to annoy a victim for a day) to 'slave auctions' (involving volunteers only) are staged as colleges vie with each other for the position of top fund-raiser.

The Lent Term also sees a spate of elections amongst the student community. Both college and university student union ballots are held and campaign banners appear throughout the colleges. Often, much time and expense is devoted by the candidates to getting themselves elected. Cambridge is developing a reputation for relative political apathy; in the 1993 elections, independent candidates were more highly favoured than those who affiliated themselves to any particular political party.

The end of the Lent Term sees its highlight for rowers, the first of the year's two 'Bumps'. To the uninitiated this is a spectacle to behold with seventeen boats, starting at one-and-a-half lengths distance apart, chasing each other up the river for four consecutive days. Each crew attempts literally to 'bump' the boat ahead before being bumped by the chasing one, and before the course is completed.

Any boats involved in a bump will change places in the division (the order in which the boats line up on the river for each day's racing). A crew that bumps on all four days gets 'blades', which means that they get to keep an oar painted up in college colours and recording the names of the rowers and the colleges bumped. In many pubs around Cambridge you will be able to see such oars displayed, gifts from the boat clubs involved.

The boat that is top of the first division obviously cannot bump anyone, so blades are also awarded to the crew who finishes the bumps at the prestigious position of Head of the River. One tradition that survives into the present day is for this crew to burn a boat and jump over it as it blazes.

In the same week as the Bumps, Cambridge's most prestigious student drama club, the Marlowe Society, puts on its annual production. Traditionally at the Arts Theatre in Cambridge, currently (July 1993) closed for refurbishment, the play is always a celebrated, heavyweight one, directed by a theatre professional. The two most recent productions have been Marlowe's *Tamburlaine*, directed by the National Theatre director Tim Supple, and Ibsen's *Peer Gynt*, directed by the Russian Irina Brown.

The start of the Spring vacation in early April sees the focal point of the Cambridge rowing year, the internationally famous Boat Race against Oxford. Held between Putney and Mortlake on the Thames in London, this televised contest is not so much an Oxbridge event as a national one. Hordes of students descend on the banks of the river for the day, filling the waterside pubs with noise and friendly rivalry. 1993's Boat Race saw Cambridge triumph against a semi-professional Oxford crew with an Olympic gold medallist, Matthew Pinsent, as their captain.

*Boat-burning at
Trinity Hall*

Apart from the Boat Race, most students will be working hard at their academic work over the Spring break, preparing for exams in the summer. The tone of the Easter Term is one of very hard work followed by a plethora of parties. The exam period starts towards the end of May, and finishes in the second week of June. Most colleges are closed or have restricted access at this time. Some subjects finish much earlier than others—English, for example, sometimes finishes two weeks before Classics—so the city can be filled with ecstasy and agony simultaneously.

Exams results, posted on boards outside the Senate House, start appearing before the end of term, at the end of the second week in June. One of the most nerve-racking experiences of a student's time at Cambridge is finding his or her name on the class-lists. British universities divide their degree results into four classes, first, upper second, lower second and third. A first or upper second is usually considered commendable.

As soon as exams are over, it is time for the students to let their hair down. The week after the end of term is known as May Week, despite the fact that it is always in June. This is a week of garden parties, cocktails, punting, picnics and Balls for those who can afford them, and most people usually find some way of celebrating. At the same time, the Footlights Revue starts its summer tour in Cambridge, warming up with a home audience before going throughout the country, including a spell on the Edinburgh Festival Fringe.

Cambridge May Balls are celebrated for their extravagance and luxury. Tickets for them become available in early April, and they are usually sold out by the middle of the Easter Term. Trinity is always the biggest, traditionally organised by the college's boat club, though many colleges would contest its claim to be the best. The spectacular setting of the

backs makes any ball held by one of the central colleges to be an unfor
gettable night—Clare College has a reputation for romance, whilst
Queens' food is always spectacular.

The sight of elegant moonlit college gardens thronged with rev
ellers in dinner-jackets and often sumptuous ballgowns is a memory o
Cambridge which seems as if it will last forever. Balls are often
themed; 1930s films, The Seven Deadly Sins and The Garden o
Delights have recently featured amongst the publicity posters. More
conventionally, big-name performers from the music and comedy
worlds such as the Bhundu Boys and Jo Brand make regular appear
ances, and other attractions range from fairground rides to hot air bal
loons. Magdalene Ball, traditionally the most extravagant, included a
flight to Paris for breakfast as part of the entertainment on one memo
rable year. With so many things to do, making it to the Survivors' photo
at six in the morning is not quite the challenge it sounds.

At the ball

Most students have left Cambridge by the end of May Week. At
the end of June, however, all those who have finished their university
courses return to receive their degrees at the Senate House. Graduands
(those about to graduate) must wear full academical dress for the grad
uation ceremony; this includes a white bow tie, a gown and an 'ermine'
hood for those receiving BA degrees. The ceremony involves grasping
one of the fingers of the Vice-Chancellor of the University whilst he
pronounces a Latin declaration. Then, you have left Cambridge
University.

Once the undergraduates have left, Cambridge becomes rather qui
eter. The city residents and graduate students remain, however, and
the city puts on its own series of festivals during the summer holidays
known as the long vacation, or 'long vac.' Following in the footsteps of
Strawberry Fair, which comes to Cambridge on the first weekend in
June, the Midsummer Fair, dating from the 13th century, arrives at the
end of the month.

Traditionally, the Cambridge Festival would take place in July
complimented by a Fringe Festival co-ordinated by the ADC Theatre
in Park Street. The festival itself has now gone into liquidation, but is
being replaced by a whole summer of events, aimed at a wider audi
ence. However, the fringe still continues with a wide range of music
and drama for two weeks in July.

The Cambridge Folk and Film Festivals also happen in July. The
Folk Festival, which had its 29th anniversary in 1993, attracts a wide
range of groups and singers, and is held over a weekend in the grounds
of Cherry Hinton Hall. Cambridge holds one of Britain's most impor
tant film festivals. In 1993 it saw the British premières of 40 different
movies during its fortnight's duration, and over 100 were shown. It is
organised by the Arts Cinema in Market passage. At the end of the
month, the city hold its own 'bumps' in which town crews compete for
the head of the river.

August is a quiet month in Cambridge, as many people go on holi
day. September, however, sees the Cambridge Fun Run and the
Autumn regatta. And in October, an entirely new set of freshers arrive
to begin the cycle again.

A hot air balloon at the 1993 Trinity May Ball

A Day in the Life of the University

There is no typical day in the life of a Cambridge student. No undergraduate's or graduate's way of life is the same, as they vary according to subject and extra-curricular interests. Whilst a diligent science student may spend all day in lecture-hall and library a history student passionate about theatre may be spending all day and all night preparing for his or her production, putting off an essay to the last possible minute. It is for this reason that this section has been called "A Day in the Life of the University"—it is an attempt to capture some of the different events going on amongst students in Cambridge.

Early morning rowing outing

5.30am The first boat crews start appearing on the river Cam. It is often difficult to find time to row, as students have many commitments during the day; some coaches, therefore, ask their oarsmen or women to get up extremely early.

8.00-8.45am Depending on their efficiency, students with lectures at 9.00 get up and have their breakfast, either in their college's hall (the cafeteria, often with a splendid dining room) or in their rooms. Some students may be woken up by a knock on the door by their 'bedder', the room-cleaners traditionally employed by the colleges. Bedders have the right (and the keys) to enter students' rooms every morning except Sunday, and the traditional 'do not disturb' sign is putting one's waste bin outside the door. Bins outside doors are, naturally, the source of much gossipamongst neighbours, who may jump to conclusions as to just why someone does not wish to be disturbed. These conclusions are quite likely to be false, as it has been calculated that half of Cambridge's students are celibate.

9.00am Lectures begin for the day. Most scientific courses, including medicine and veterinary medicine, require that their students attend a full day of lectures, sometimes seven hours' worth. Each lecture is one hour long. Arts faculties, such as those of History or English, put on lectures, but students are often much more selective about those which they attend. This is because there are usually fewer that are relevant to a particular student's chosen topics. Often, arts students will opt to spend the morning reading, either in the library or in their room, rather than go to a lecture.

1.00pm Whilst lunch in Hall in the colleges will have started at around 12.30, one o' clock sees the second bicycle rush hour of the day (the first was at 9.00) as everybody returns from the lecture halls to find themselves something to eat.

2.00pm Supervisions usually happen in the afternoon rather than the morning. As a student may have three or four a week, whatever subject (s)he does, they are a regular feature of life. Lectures, practicals and classes continue, for some, until 6.00.

2.15pm Inter-college sports matches are usually held in the afternoons. A wide range of sports are played, from Netball to Rugby Union, and the contests are often hard-fought. Particularly sporty colleges are Downing and Hughes Hall (for rugby) and Jesus and Trinity Hall (for rowing). Most colleges have their own sports grounds in and around the city.

5.45pm-7.00pm Cafeteria dinner is available in Hall. A majority of students eat in Hall at some stage during the day, as it is usually the cheapest way of getting food.

7.30pm Formal Hall starts. An occasion unique to a few British universities, this was traditionally the smart dinner of the evening, a three-course waiter-served meal by candlelight. Now, Formal Hall is a smarter, longer and slightly more expensive alternative to cafeteria dinner, usually only chosen by students who have something to celebrate. Gowns must be worn to Formal Hall, but there are few other dress regulations, which often leads to the slightly comic sight of a gown over jeans and T-shirt. Some colleges only have Formal Hall one or two nights a week.

7.30-8.00pm Student plays start at the Playroom in St Edward's Passage and the ADC Theatre in Park Street, the oldest university playhouse in Britain. "The ADC" is the centre of Cambridge's drama scene. Student plays are usually plentiful and of an extremely high quality, and sometimes written by undergraduates. Several Cambridge drama groups annually put on shows at the Edinburgh Fringe Festival, often to critical acclaim. The University has produced Emma Thompson, Oscar-winning actress, and the celebrated director Sir Peter Hall, amongst others.

Formal Hall at Trinity Hall

8.00pm A concert may start at the University's West Road concert hall. Performances by the University Music Society (UMS) are usually the most accomplished, but individual and college groups often contain considerable talent.

8.15pm Other University societies, from the Jewish Society to the Sports Parachuting Association, hold speaker meetings or get-togethers during the evening. The former can vary from the downright dull to the absorbingly interesting, whilst the latter are often held in pubs.

9.00pm If it is a Friday or Saturday night, this is the time at which college discos, known as 'bops' or 'sweatys' start, although they never fill up until around 11.00. Fitzwilliam College is well-known for its bi-termly 'Fitz entz', often with well-known disc jockeys, and Trinity's

Burning the midnight oil

'Sweatys' are usually packed, serving cheap, ferocious cocktails such as 'Sex on the Backs'.

10.00pm Again, if it is Friday or Saturday, undergraduate parties begin at this time. For some reason, private parties in Cambridge never seem to start until 10.00, and reach a peak between midnight and one am. Parties can be held by entire staircases in a college, or by an individual. Theming of parties is popular, from 'tacos and tequila' to 'headgear essential.' Many an undergraduate's Friday or Saturday night is spent in regal progress from party to party and from college to college. Parties carry one wrinkle, however—permission usually has to be sought from the Senior Tutor or Lay Dean (the Fellows responsible for maintaining discipline) and many colleges' porters seem to take pride in shutting down illegal or over-long gatherings. Some invitations have been known to state '10pm until the porters'.

The Dangerous Pastries, stars of a late night comedy show at the Playroom in 1993

10.15pm College bars start to fill up, as students gather for a late-night drink after their evening's work or other activities. The bar is usually the social centre of the college, combined with the Junior Combination Room (always shortened to JCR, and traditional term for the undergraduates' common room.) Most students can be sure of seeing their friends in one of these two places. Graduates usually have their own common rooms (Middle Combination Rooms or MCRs), and Fellows the Senior Combination Rooms (surprisingly shortened to SCRs), but in some colleges undergraduates, graduates and Fellows rub shoulders nightly at the bar. College bars vary enormously, but all rigorously maintain the rule of serving only college members and their guests.

11.00pm Lateshows start at ADC and Playroom theatres. Often more avant-garde and risqué than the earlier 'mainshows', lateshows can vary from dance performances to productions of little-known plays. Footlights traditionally holds its bi-termly 'smokers' at this time in the ADC, comedy revues for which auditions, open to all comers, are held a few nights previously. Their standard is usually high.

2.00am Those parties that are quiet or lucky enough not to have been 'busted' by the porters peter out, as the revellers find their way back to bed. Earlier in the century, students were obliged to be back in their rooms before a certain (early) time in the evening, or face severe penalties. Now, some colleges still maintain a system where 'late keys' must be signed out of the porters' lodge to gain re-admission after a certain time, but the most that a student can usually expect from coming back late into his or her college is a ticking off from the porters.

3.00am Those students who have delayed the writing of their essays to the last minute, or who simply have a very largeamount of work to do, can be found working into the small hours. 'Burning the midnight oil' due to what is known as an 'essay crisis', is something that most students will experience at some time in their Cambridge career.

A Dictionary of Cambridge Slang

A long way: anywhere more than five minutes' walk away

Backs, *n*: the area between the backs of the colleges and Queens' Road, close to the Cam

Bedder, *n*: Member of college staff (now always female) who makes students' beds and cleans their rooms. Takes no interest in the nocturnal activities of students (?)

Boatie, *n*: Rower, usually with same characteristics as rugger-bugger

Bop, *a.k.a.* **Sweaty**, *a.k.a.* **Event**, *n*: disco, sometimes with food, always with drink

Ministry of Truth or **UL**, *n*: The University Library (because of its brutal architecture)

Bumps, *n*: Complicated rowing races in which each college boat tries to catch up with the next

Cambridge (*as in* 'so Cambridge'), *adj* :used to describe something that is meant to characterise student life, *usu.* with sense of somebody taking something to extremes

Catz, *n*: St Catharine's College

Cindy's, *n*: reference to Cinderella Rockerfellas, nighclub, *usu.* derogatory

Compsci, *n*: Student reading computer science, *usu.* derogatory. See **natsci**

Confie, *n*: conference delgate (*usu.* used in combination with irritation about 'how delegates take over colleges outside term')

Desmond (*also 'dezzy'*), *n*: Lower second in exams, usually finals. From Desmond Tutu (two-two)

Dosser, *n*: Lazy person (from 'doss-house')

Dweeb, *n* (rare)=narg

Emma, *n*: Emmanuel College

Entz, *n (pl)*: Entertainments (*usu.* provided by college **JCR**s)

Fitz, *n*: 1. Fitzwilliam College. 2. **The ~** The Fitzwilliam Museum

Gardies, *n*: The Gardenia late-night takeaway, in Rose Crescent

Grad-pad, *n*: The University Centre used by graduates for food and accommodation (from Graduate + pad)

Gyp room, *n*: Small kitchen for student use, habitually with a few rings and no oven. (from gyp, obsolete term for male bedder)

Hack, *n*: Excessively motivated, often selfish, student who attempts to get to the top of undergraduate politics or journalism. Also **to ~**, verb

JCR, *n*: Junior Combination Room. Either an undergraduate common room, or the students elected to look after undergraduate affairs by their peers

King Street Run, *n*: Tour of the King St pubs in each of which the participants must drink a pint

Mathmo, *n*: Student reading Mathematics

May Week, *n*: Week in June (confusingly) when **May Balls** occur (from original month when balls were held)

May Ball, *n*: Very, very big and expensive party to celebrate end of exams, usually with several hundred guests. College-based, they feature everything from bouncy castles to Bailey's Irish Cream

Muso, *n*: 1. Student reading music. 2. Musician (often one and the same)

Narg, 1. *n*: A student (*usu.* male) who is hard-working, boring and socially inept; typically physically unattractive and badly-dressed. 2. *v.i.* **To ~** (*perh. f.* imitating narg's manner of speech)

Natsci, *n*: student reading natural sciences, *usu.* derogatory, hinting that they are nargs

Pidge or **P/hole**, *n*: student's mail pigeon-hole (*abbrev.*)

Plodge, *n*: porters' lodge (*abbrev.*)

Quiche, *v.i.*: to wimp out, to be cowardly and weak

Rag, *n*: students' fund-raising charity. Also ~ Week (from *obs.* Rag=jape)

Rugger-bugger, *n*: Rugby-player, esp. one given to rowdy behaviour and drunkenness

Shark, *v.t.*: to pursue members of the opposite sex unscrupulously

Spod, *n*=narg

Squash, *n*: open meeting at start of year (*usu.* alcoholic) of a college or university society for the purposes of recruiting new members

Thesp, 1. *n*: student actor or actress, *usu.* with associated pretentiousness and tendency to show off. 2. *v.i.* to act 3. *v.i.* to behave in a **thespy** (*adj.*) manner

Tit Hall, *n*: Trinity Hall (*abbrev.*)

Trash, *v.t.*: to ransack a room or divest it of its contents, *usu.* after party

Typewriter, *n*: Christ's College New Court (from its shape)

Vac, *n*: vacation (abbrev.)

WALKS

Please note: All of the walks in this guidebook start and finish in front of King's College Porters' Lodge, in King's Parade. This is marked with a 'W' on the map inside the back cover, and a photo can be found on page 40, the next page

Walk One:
The Riverside Colleges

Allow one and a half hours

Facing King's College Porters' Lodge, turn right along King's Parade. Just after King's College Chapel on your left, you will see a large neo-classical building, the Senate House, and opposite it on the right, Great St. Mary's Church (p. 88).

A large university assembly hall, the Senate House fulfils a number of functions, most importantly as an examination hall and as the place where degrees are given out at the end of a student's time at Cambridge. The boards ouside the Senate House are covered with sheets of examination results towards the end of the Easter Term (end of May-beginning of June).

The Senate House was the scene of the most famous undergraduate joke derived from the sport of 'night-climbing' amidst the roofs of Cambridge. On one occasion in June 1958, the city awoke to find an old Austin van sitting on the roof of the Senate House. This feat was most recently matched by those who managed to scale King's Chapel one night and fix a banner 38 feet long reading "Peace in Vietnam" between the towers facing King's Parade. The climbers responsible for this feat were later caught by the Police after climbing onto the Senate House roof, and 'sent down' (expelled from the University).

Go through the traffic barriers into a cobbled area, with the Senate House on your left. In front of you is Gonville and Caius College (p. 19), always shortened to just 'Caius' (pronounced Keys, as it is the Latin version of the name of the co-founder, Dr John Keys). Veer to the left and turn left down a small cobbled alley, Senate House Pasage, keeping the Senate House on your left. Follow this alley to the end.

As you pass down the alley, notice the elaborate gate on your right. This is Caius' Gate of Honour, crowned by sundials, and made to an Italian model. It is the third of the three gates which a student at Caius would go through in his time at the college, as designed by Dr John Keys. The others were the gates of Humility and Virtue.

At the end of Senate House Passage, you will notice an alley to the left. If you go down here, you will come to Clare College (p. 16) on your right, and the visitors' entrance to King's College Chapel.

If you wish to carry on with the route of this walk, however, turn right at the end of Senate House Passage, passing the entrance to Trinity Hall College (p. 19) on the left. Shortly afterwards, turn left again down Garret Hostel Lane. There should be 'To The River' marked in chalk on one of the walls of this lane, with an arrow pointing down it.

Caius College
Gate of Honour

King's College Porters' Lodge, the starting-point for all walks (map over)

Follow this lane over the steep Garret Hostel Bridge, and to just before it reaches a large main road (Queens' Road), when you will notice two parallel paths off to the left. Take the first of these paths, keeping the trees and the road to your right. You are now on Cambridge's famous 'Backs', named because you can see the 'backs' of the colleges from this area. Carry on along the Backs until you see the splendour of King's College over a field to your left. If you see people without feet, but standing up holding poles, moving slowly but regularly along in front of the lawns next to the chapel, you are seeing people punting, not hallucinating!

The path will end in a line of barriers just after you see King's chapel, and you will notice the back entrance to the college on your left. The path will have led you onto the pavement beside Queens' Road.

There are two small crests on the gate, one with three roses in the bottom half of the shield, and another with three fleur de lis. The crest with the roses on is that of King's; the crest to the right of it, with the lilies, is that of Eton College, the famous English 'public school'. King's and Eton are twin foundations, founded to complement each other—scholars from the school were supposed to continue their education at the college.

Go through or around the barriers and take the footpath which crosses the green space diagonally to the left of you. (If this is a problem for wheelchairs, follow Queens' Road and take the first left down Silver Street, following the instructions from the next paragraph.) Follow this path until you reach the barriers at the end, and then turn left onto Silver Street.

Follow Silver Street over the Cam. As you pass over the bridge, look to your left, and you will see Queens' famous Mathematical Bridge. One apocryphal student story relates that the bridge would stand up on its own without the bolts holding the bridge's beams to each other, but undergraduates were so adept at taking it apart that it had to be fixed together!

Shortly after you have crossed the river, you will see Queens' Lane off to your left, which leads to the visitors' entrance to Queens' College. If you are not visiting Queens', carry on up Silver Street until it turns sharply to the right into Trumpington Street, next to Ede and Ravenscroft, the gentleman's outfitter's shop on the corner.

At this junction, turn left into Trumpington Street. You will pass St Catharine's College on your left, and Corpus Christi College on your right. Follow this road until you see King's Porters' Lodge on your left.

Queens' College
Mathematical Bridge

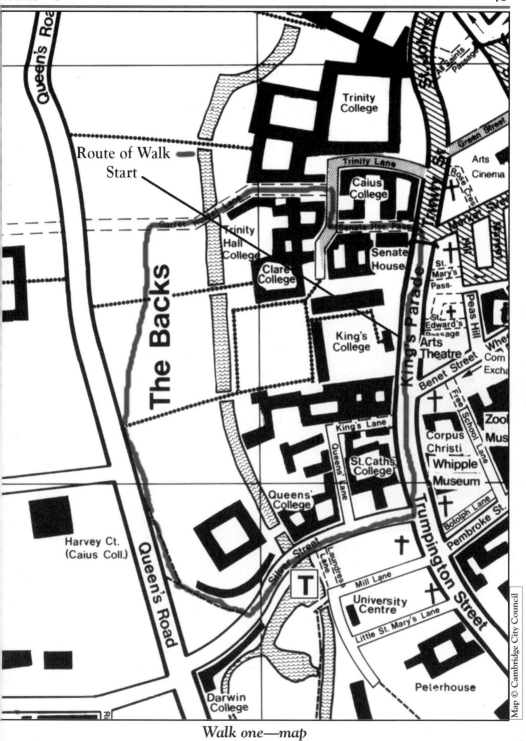

Route of Walk
Start

Walk one—map

Walk Two:
Further Colleges and the
Town Centre

Allow one and a half hours

Facing King's College Porters' Lodge, turn left along King's Parade. Carry on straight ahead as it turns into Trumpington Street opposite Vivat Brasserie. You will pass Corpus Christi College on your left and St Catharine's College on your right. Soon, you will reach a junction, with St Bene't's church on your left (p. 88).

At the junction, carry on along the left side of Trumpington Street, the road straight ahead, for a few metres until you see St Botolph's Lane off to the left. Follow this small, attractive road to its end.

Next, veer right and you will reach Pembroke Street. Turn left, and follow this road right to its end at a T-junction and traffic lights. You will find that its name changes to Downing Street after 20 metres or so—do not be alarmed, but carry on along it.

When you reach the end of this road, you will see a large classical entrance over the road in front of you. This is Emmanuel College, famous for its former student John Harvard, founder of the Massachusetts University, and, amongst contemporary University students, for its ducks. (See p. 23 for more details)

Turn left at the T-junction into St Andrew's Street. When the road bends around to the right, carry on straight ahead over the cobbles, following St Andrew's Street. After a while, the road will fork, and you will see an ornate gatehouse on the right. This is the entrance to Christ's College (see p. 22 for more details). Take the left-hand fork.

You will notice that you are either passing through or going around a set of gates. These, and the various other traffic obstacles that you will see at certain junctions around the city, are part of Cambridge City Council's controversial scheme which bans bicycles and traffic from the centre of town. Most spectacular are the obstacles which rise from and descend into the road to allow particular vehicles access to the restricted area.

Follow Sidney Street as it bends slightly to the right. When Market Street joins from the left just after the branch of Woolworth's, carry on straight ahead along Sidney Street. About 40 metres or so along this road you will see a college gate to your right and Sainsbury's supermarket opposite, on your left.

The college on your right is Sidney Sussex College, sometimes known to students as 'Sidney Sainsbury's', because of its proximity to the supermarket. Perhaps fedup with this nickname, students from the college once painted a pedestrian crossing across Sidney Street from the entrance of their college to the entrance of Sainsbury's, and proceeded to use it until it was removed.

The front of Emmanuel College

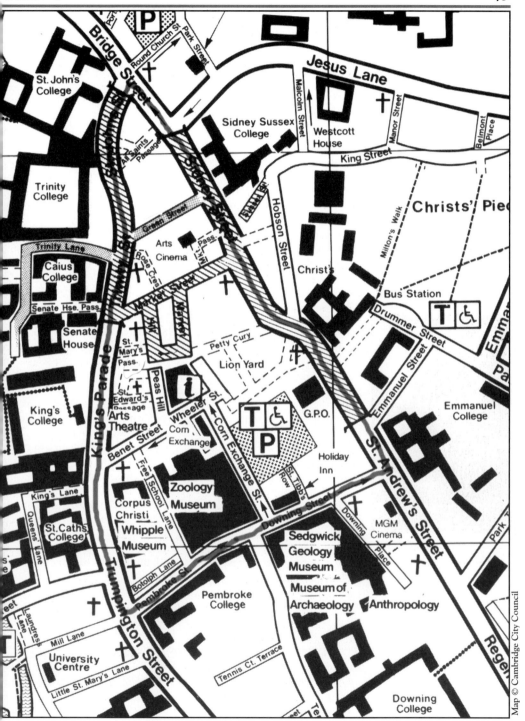

Walk two—map

When Sidney Street reaches a junction with a road that comes from the right and then bends round to carry on straight in front of you, follow the flow of traffic and go straight on into Bridge Street. After 40 metres or so, you will see church on your right. This is The Round Church (the origin of its name is self-evident). For more details, see p. 88.

To the right of the Round Church as you face it you will see a small alleyway, and a notice which shows the way to the Cambridge Union Society. One of the largest and oldest student societies (it was founded in 1815), it provides a forum for political and social debate. 'The Union', as it is known, still attracts many politicians and personalities to speak at its weekly debates. Recent visitors have included the Dalai Lama of Tibet and Andrea Dworkin, the radical feminiSt

The tradition of Union politics is so strong that it has been suggested that there is something of a 'Cambridge Mafia' in the British Conservative Party today. While Norman Lamont has recently resigned, his contemporaries John Selwyn Gummer, Michael Howard, and Kenneth Clarke still remain in the Cabinet. All four of these politicians were Union Society presidents in successive years from 1961 to 1964.

Carry on a little way along Bridge Street until St John's Street branches off to your left. Turn into St John's Street. On your right, you will notice the immense edifice of St John's College chapel, and further along, the entrance to the college (p. 21). Carry on along St John's Street and you will come to Trinity College Great Gate, again on your right.

If you look up at the statue of Henry VIII, founder of the college, in the centre of the gate, you will notice that he is not holding a sceptre in his right hand, but a chair-leg. This is testimony to the dangerous undergraduate sport of night-climbing, the scaling of University buildings under the cover of darkness. The earliest recorded night-climber was not a student, but was nevertheless involved with Trinity College. Some time in the early 19th century, when it was the fashion for fellows to wear wigs, the barber serving Trinity was bribed by undergraduates to climb up the college Library and put the best wigs belonging to the senior Fellows on the head of the statues facing the Hall.

St John's College Chapel

Continue along the same street, which has now become Trinity Street. You will pass Heffers, the city's most encyclopaedic bookshop, on your left, and some way further along, Gonville and Caius (pronounced "keys") College on your right (p. 19). Carry on along Trinity Street until you see King's College Chapel over to the right as you reach the junction with St Mary's Street. Cross over the road, through the barriers, and head up King's Parade, remaining on the left side of the road.

Just before you reach King's College you will pass Ryder and Amies, a gentleman's outfitters. If you look in the bottom of the windows of the shop, you will see a number of noticeboards. The University sports clubs have displayed their notices in these windows since the turn of the century, a practice which reflects both the deep-rooted history of university sport, and its essentially unchanged nature.

Carry on along King's Parade, and you will find yourself at King's College Porters' Lodge once more.

The statue of Henry VIII, Trinity Great Gate

Walk Three: Grantchester and the Meadows

Allow at least four hours

G rantchester, a place of winding streets and thatched roofs, has long been a retreat for students. Just far enough out of Cambridge to feel 'away', undergraduates take to the village for a quiet drink in one of the pubs, as a destination for a long punting trip, or purely for a bit of countryside. The village's name is derived from the Cam's other name, the 'Granta'. The poet Rupert Brooke nostalgically recalled the two years (1910-1912) he spent in the 17th century Old Vicarage in his well-known poem 'Grantchester', and the house is now home to the popular novelist Jeffrey Archer.

An excellent place to stop and rest once you have reached Grantchester is the Orchard Tea Gardens (directions are in the text of the walk). A place where Wittgenstein, Virginia Woolf and John Maynard Keynes have taken tea amongst the trees, its slightly bohemian atmosphere and comfortable deck-chairs are ideal for relaxation on a fine summer's day (inside seating is available when the weather is unkind). The Tea Garden is, sadly, in danger through debt and developers; hopefully, it will survive during the lifetime of this guidebook.

If you are in search of stronger refreshment, Grantchester offers three good pubs, The Green Man, The Red Lion, and The Rupert Brooke, all of which also serve food. The best views are available from The Rupert Brooke. All three pubs are on the route of the walk below.

This walk takes the visitor on the classic way to the village, through Grantchester Meadows beside the Cam.

F acing King's Porters' Lodge, turn left and follow King's Parade and Trumpington Street to the junction with Silver Street, just by St Botolph's church. On your way, you will pass St Catharine's College on your right and Corpus Christi College on your left.

Keep going straight ahead over the junction, crossing onto the right side of the road, where you will see a large Gothic building. This is the site of the old Cambridge University Press, now the Pitt Building. Walking to the far end of this building you will come to Mill Lane on your right. Follow Mill Lane past the University Careers Service and the Department of Pure Maths until you reach the Mill Pub, a favourite with students in the summer when they have finished their exams.

The Mill pub

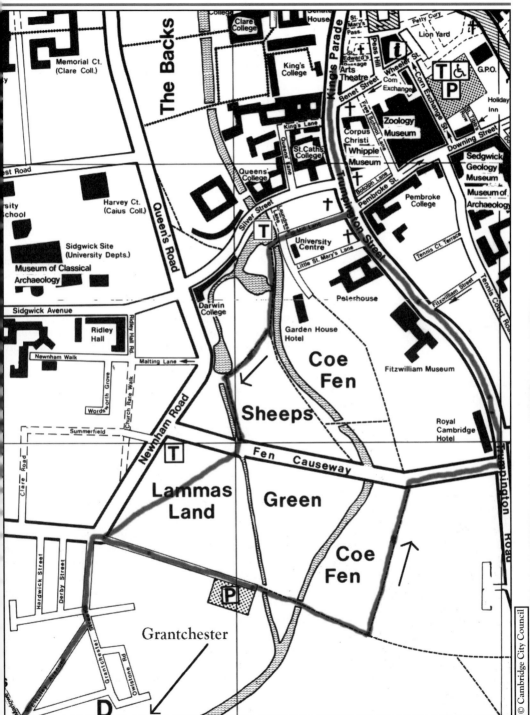

Walk three—central Cambridge section map

Opposite the pub you will see a gate and bridge over the Cam. Cross the river and follow the path beside it, which veers to the left. When the path forks, take the right-hand path. Walk across two bridges, reaching a junction of paths. Take the left-hand path alongside a stream on the right. Cross the main road by the pedestrian crossing and continue across the green on the path in front of you, named Lammas land, until you come to another main road. Turn left along this road and carry on straight ahead into Grantchester Street close by.

Follow Grantchester Street until you reach the third road on the right, Eltisley Avenue. Go to the end of Eltisley Avenue. Take the road straight in front of you which veers slightly to the right. Carry on into a gravelled car park, following the Public Footpath sign to Grantchester. At the end of the car park, take a narrow hedged byway which leads to Granchester Meadows through a gate. Follow the long tarmac path through the meadows through three more gates.

Carry on straight ahead through another gate until you reach a main road. You have reached Grantchester. The Orchard Tea Garden, an excellent place to stop and have a cool drink, is a little way along the road to the left (entrance for cars and the disabled a little further, around the corner).

To carry on with the main walk, turn right at the main road and continue until you reach the Green Man pub and a small village green. The Red Lion is a little further along the small road to the right, past the Green Man.

At this point, the disabled will need to retrace their journey to return to Cambridge.

Carry on along the main road until you reach the Rupert Brooke pub on the right. Go to the extreme left-hand end of the pub's garden and car park and you will find a stile back into the meadows. Head straight ahead across the meadow until you reach the path once more. Turn left onto the path and retrace your steps as far as the city centre end of Grantchester Street.

At this point, take the road to your right, at right-angles to Grantchester Street, with yellow lines along it. It is signposted "The Granta Housing Trust". Follow this road until you see an entrance to a car park on your right. Take the path in front of you through the barriers and over a black bridge. Carry on, veering slightly left along the path until you come to a junction of paths just before a boathouse. Take the left-hand path around the boathouse and continue alongside the river until you reach the main road.

Cross the road and turn right onto the pavement. Carry on along this road until you reach a set of roundabouts. Turn left at the first roundabout and the carry straight on along Trumpington Street. Follow Trumpington Street, passing the Fitzwilliam Museum, Peterhouse and Pembroke, until you reach the Pitt building once more. Retrace your steps along Trumpington Street and King's Parade to King's Porters' Lodge.

The Green Man Pub, Grantchester

Grantchester Meadows

Walk Four:
Jesus, Magdalene and
Green Spaces

Allow 2 hours (2 1/2 if you choose to pass Magdalene College and climb Castle Mound). The ascent of Castle Hill is difficult for the disabled.

Great St. Mary's Church

Facing King's Porters' Lodge, turn right along King's Parade. Soon, you will notice Great St Mary's Church, the University Church, on your right (see p. 88). Just after Great St Mary's, go through the traffic barriers and turn right down Market Street. Carry on down Market Street, passing Cambridge's Market on your right.

Market Street veers sharply to the left close to the stationery department of Heffers. Follow the road round. Its name will change to Sidney Street, but carry on straight ahead, past Sidney Sussex College on your right (p. 22) and the branch of Sainsbury's supermarket opposite. Soon after you have passed the entrance to Sidney Sussex, Sidney Street will come to the point at which a road comes in from the right and continues straight ahead.

Turn right down the road coming in from the right, Jesus Lane, crossing onto the left side of the road. Carry on along Jesus Lane until you reach some traffic lights.

If you look to your left, you will see the ADC Theatre. The home of Cambridge's flourishing student drama scene, it shows two plays a week during term-time. Student actors and actresses at Cambridge are known as 'Thesps' (from thespian), and are caricatured amongst undergraduates as insincere and exhibitionist. Nevertheless, Cambridge theatre is usually of a very high quality, and the ADC is definitely worth a visit.

Cross straight over the road and the traffic lights, and carry on along the left side of Jesus Lane for about 300 metres, passing Marshalls garage on your left.

Opposite the tall spire of the church on the right hand side of the road, you will notice a black wrought-iron gate to your left, and a long walled passage behind it. This is the entrance to Jesus College (p. 22). The walkway is known as 'the chimney'.

If you are not visiting Jesus, carry on along Jesus lane another 200 metres until you reach a roundabout. Keeping to the left-hand side of the road, follow the pavement as it turns along Victoria Avenue, the first turning to the left out of the roundabout. Continue straight along this avenue of trees for about 300 metres, until you reach a pedestrian crossing where the road bends.

As you pass along Victoria Avenue, notice the green space to your right, on the other side of the road. This is Midsummer Common, where a fair has been held since the Middle Ages. The buildings on

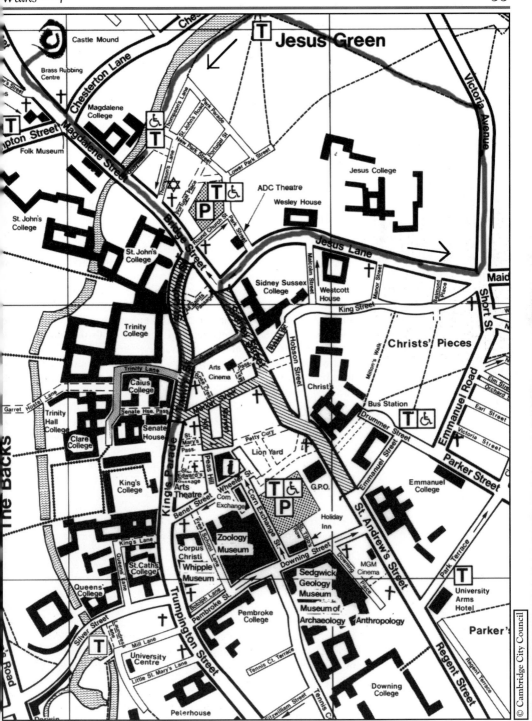

Walk four—map

The avenue of trees across Jesus Green

the far side of the common, a little to your right as you go up Victoria Avenue, are college and University boathouses.

At the pedestrian crossing, turn left through some metal barriers onto a path across a park in front of you, Jesus Green. The path is another avenue of trees.

Carry on straight ahead down the avenue, ignoring the path which crosses it half-way across Jesus Green, until you reach a bridge over the Cam and a lock. Turn left onto the path which follows the left bank of the Cam. After 50 or so metres, the path forks, with the tarmac veering off to the left and another path turning right, through some barriers, and keeping close to the Cam.

Take the right-hand path, keeping the Spade and Becket pub to your left, and moving onto a wooden walkway. Follow the walkway and the Cam until you reach Magdalene Bridge and Bridge Street.

As you walk along the walkway, you will notice a garden on the other side of the river. This is Magdalene College's Fellows' Garden. Most colleges have 'Fellows' Gardens', which may or may not be open to undergraduates. One college's Fellows' Garden even contains an outdoor swimming pool.

If you wish to visit Magdalene College, or climb up Castle Mound, then turn right over Magdalene Bridge into Magdalene Street. About 30 metres along Magdalene Street, to the right as you go up it, is the entrance to Magdalene College (p. 21.). To get to Castle Mound, carry on up Magdalene Street. At the traffic lights, carry on straight up Castle Hill, ensuring that you are on the right hand side of the road. Just after you pass the Castle Inn on the right hand side of the road, you will see a small path to the right. Take this path, which crosses the car park of Shire Hall, the large building to the left as you turn onto it. (Shire Hall is the headquarters of Cambridgeshire County Council.). On the right, you will see Castle Mound and the path which leads up to the top of it. Retrace your steps and carry on back over Magdalene Bridge onto Bridge Street. Ignore the next paragraph, and then follow the remainder of the walk back to King's.

If you wish to return to King's Parade, turn left at Magdalene Bridge, down Bridge Street.

Follow this road until you see St John's Street off to the right, a road which is surfaced in brick, and which is opposite the Round Church on the left.

Turn into St John's Street. On your right, you will notice the immense edifice of St John's College chapel, and further along, the entrance to the college (page 21). Carry on along St John's Street and you will come to Trinity College on your right (p. 19).

Continue along the same street, which has now become Trinity Street. You will pass Heffers, the city's most encyclopaedic bookshop, on your left, and some way further along, Gonville and Caius (pronounced "keys") College on your right (p. 19). Carry on along Trinity Street until you see King's College Chapel over to the right as you reach the junction with St Mary's Street. Cross over the road, through the barriers, and head up King's Parade until you find yourself at King's College Porters' Lodge once more.

THE GUIDE

Where to go in Cambridge

Cambridge has a lot to offer beyond the confines of the college courts. The city has a long and complex history of its own, and this is reflected in the enormous variety of buildings and its twisting mediaeval passageways and lanes. There is much to do and see around and about Cambridge. Here is a selection of the essentials.

Approximate times of Full University Terms:

Michaelmas	Early October-Early December
Lent	Late January-Mid March
Easter	Late April-Early June

Guided Tours

The best way to see the city's major sights is to take a guided tour. Groups wishing to visit the Colleges must register with the Tourist Information Centre and be accompanied by a registered Blue Badge Cambridge Guide.

Walking Tours

Tickets and information from the Tourist Information Centre, Wheeler Street. Telephone (0223) 322640

Tours go very regularly in the summer, and twice daily in the winter months, departing from the Information Centre. They include visits to college grounds, with an informed commentary from a trained guide.

Bus Tours

Tickets and information from Guide Friday, Cambridge Railway Station. Tel. (0223) 62444

Tours of the city, taking in the American Cemetery at Madingley, run regularly in the summer, every 10-15 minutes, in the spring and autumn, every 20 minutes, and in the winter months, every hour. Bus tours, which include a commentary on the sights, are a good way for the visitor in a hurry to see the city.

Museums and Galleries

As a great seat of learning, the University runs several museums for the benefit of its students. In addition, there are a number of museums and exhibitions charting the development of the city, and several excellent galleries. *All information is subject to change.*

THE CAMBRIDGE AND COUNTY FOLK MUSEUM
2, Castle Street
Tel (0223) 355159
Open: April-Sept: Mon-Sat 10.30am-5.00pm
*   Sun 2.00pm-5.00pm*
*   Oct-Mar: Closed Mondays; otherwise the same.*
Admission: Adults £1.00, Concessions 50p

The Folk Museum inhabits what was once an inn called 'The White Horse'. It is crammed with artefacts from Cambridge and the surrounding area, all of which would have been used in daily life during the past few hundred years. Exhibits include an entire 18th century shop-front, and the standard weights and measures dating from the time when the University ruled the city.

THE CAMBRIDGE DARKROOM
Dales Brewery, Gwydir Street
Tel. (0223) 350275
Open (gallery): Tue-Sun 2-6pm
Admission free

As its name suggests, the Cambridge Darkroom specialises in photography as an art form. Its aim is to encourage new artists, and it achieves this aim with an accessibility to be envied by larger and longer-established rivals. The Darkroom also runs talks and photographic workshops throughout the year, and provides darkroom facilities for amateur photographers.

THE FITZWILLIAM MUSEUM
Trumpington Street
Tel. (0223) 332900
Tue-Fri: Lower Gallery open 10am-2pm; Upper Gallery open 2-5pm
Sat & Sun: Both galleries open 2.15-5pm
The disabled should ring in advance for access on weekends
Admission free

The 'Fitz' is the University's art museum, and dates from 1816. The building is the work of George Basevi, who died before it was completed. The original collections of the founder, the seventh Viscount Fitzwilliam, have grown over the years. They now range from Egyptian, Greek and Roman antiquities to paintings by the French Impressionists. The library ranges from illuminated manuscripts to literary curios such as the first draft of Keats' *Ode to a Nightingale*. Works on display include Rembrandt's 'Portrait of a Man' and Titian's 'Venus and Cupid with a Lute Player.' The Upper Galleries are mainly given over to paintings, the Lower to antiquities.

Lions guard the
Fitzwilliam Museum

Art on display at Kettle's Yard

KETTLE'S YARD
Northampton Street
Tel. (0223) 352124
House open daily 2-4pm
Admission free
Closed between Christmas and New Year

Kettle's Yard is a unique collection of modern sculptures, paintings and drawings, donated to the University by Jim Ede in 1966, complete with the house which he furnished with them. Attached to the house is a gallery which usually exhibits modern art or craft works, but it is closed until Spring 1994.

THE MUSEUM OF CLASSICAL ARCHAEOLOGY
Sidgwick Avenue
Tel. (0223) 335155
Open Mon-Fri 9-5pm, plus Sat 9am - 1pm during University Terms
Admission free
Disabled people are advised to telephone in advance

This museum, house in the new Department of Classics building, boasts a collection of more than 500 casts of Greek and Roman sculptures, reliefs and statues. The museum is very much a working one, with exhibits clearly displayed to aid study.

THE SCOTT POLAR RESEARCH MUSEUM
Lensfield Road
Tel. (0223) 336540
Open Mon-Sat 2.30-4pm
Closed some bank holidays
Admission free
Good disabled access

The Scott Polar Research Institute is a memorial to the Antarctic explorer Captain Scott and his companions, who died during their epic race to reach the South Pole. On display are relics from his expeditions—including a sledge and eskimo artefacts—and exhibits explaining current polar research.

THE SEDGWICK MUSEUM OF GEOLOGY
Downing Site, Downing Street
Tel. (0223) 333456
Open Mon-Fri 9am-1pm and 2-5pm, Sat 10am-1pm
Closed during university vacations
Admission free
Poor disabled access, but telephone the museum in advance and they can help

Based on the collection of fossils started by Adam Sedgwick (Woodwardian Professor of Geology until 1873) this well-organised museum sports the skeleton of an iguanadon, an Irish Elk, and a hippopotamus—the last excavated at Barrington, near Cambridge. The museum also houses the oldest intact geological collection in the world, gathered by Dr John Woodward (1665-1728), and boasts a fossil of the largest spider ever found—36cm across.

THE UNIVERSITY MUSEUM OF ARCHAEOLOGY AND ANTHROPOLOGY
Downing Street
Open Mon-Fri 2-4pm, Sat 10.30am-12.30pm
Admission free, but donations welcome

The multitude of exhibits spans the globe, representing American, African, Pacific and South-East Asian cultures, as well as covering the Cambridge area.

THE UNIVERSITY MUSEUM OF ZOOLOGY
New Museums Site, Downing Street
Tel. (0223) 336600
Open Mon-Fri 2.15-4.45pm
Closed on public holidays
Admission free
Disabled access ramp

A collection representing the whole spectrum of animal life. Exhibits include fossils of now-extinct species, as well as preserved mammals, birds, insects and marine life.

THE WHIPPLE MUSEUM OF THE HISTORY OF SCIENCE
Free School Lane
Tel. (0223) 334540
Open Mon-Sat 2-4pm
Closed Bank Holidays
Admission free
Disabled access by arrangement

The museum is based on a collection of scientific instruments amassed by R S Whipple, which was given to the University in 1944. On display are many fascinating devices, including a clockwork model of the solar system dating from around 1750, early surveying instruments, microscopes and telescopes, and electrostatic generators. The Museum is holding an exhibition called "The Empire of Physics" until November 1993.

Scenic views of the city

The best place to look out over Cambridge's roofs is from the top of the University church, Great St Mary's, in King's Parade, open most days during the year. It is also possible to climb Castle Mound, on Castle Hill (close to Shire Hall). See walk four for more details.

A view from the Backs

Parks and Gardens

There are many lovely open spaces around the city centre. Jesus Green, between Jesus College and the Cam (access from Bridge Street, Chesterton Road and Victoria Avenue) is the largest and offers a delightful riverside walk and is an ideal spot for picnics. Just across Victoria Avenue is Midsummer Common, where the city's spectacular Guy Fawkes Night fireworks display is held every November. The Midsummer Fair held annually on the common has roots in mediaeval times. Parker's Piece, off Regent Street (near the University Arms Hotel) makes another excellent picnicking place. The lamp-post in the middle of Parker's Piece is cynically known amongst students as 'Reality Checkpoint', as it is felt that it marks the south-eastern boundary between town and gown.

Sheep's Green (access by the bridge at the end of Mill Lane) is a favourite place to stop and picnic, as it is right next to the Mill pub, and close to the river. Lammas Land, a little further along the towpath, can be quieter during the summer. For the most adventurous, the wide expanses of Grantchester Meadows (see the *Walks* section) are a favourite place for students to relax.

It should be remembered that colleges discourage picknickers in their grounds. However, there are grassy areas along the Backs which lend themselves to a pleasant break from the bustle of the sightseeing trail. Although busy Queens' Road is nearby, the area between King's back gate and the rear of Queens' College can be quite tranquil.

At the end of the summer term, during 'May Week', many colleges hold plays in their Fellows' Gardens. Often of a very high standard, they can be magical. Queens' College Cloister Court is probably the best venue, and usually puts on a Shakespeare play (in 1993, it was *A Midsummer Night's Dream*). Some colleges' Fellows' Gardens are open during the summer under the National Gardens Scheme. Watch out for notices giving details.

UNIVERSITY BOTANIC GARDEN
Entrances on Hills Road, Trumpington Street and Bateman Street
Tel. (0223) 336265
Open from 8am, Mon-Sun throughout the year. Closing time depends on time of dusk.
Admission free except on Sundays (£1 for adults)
Good access for the disabled

The 40 acres of gardens are delightfully laid out, with a variety of lawns, flowerbeds, plant-houses and an eye-catching rockery. The collections are second only to those at Kew in botanic importance, and are an excellent place to relax.

The garden also offers a picnic area (close to the Hills Road entrance), refreshments, and a gift shop.

Midsummer Common—in a less-than-walkable state

Entertainments

Theatre

Aside from various in-college theatre stages, Cambridge has four main drama venues. Most well-known, and the home of the Footlights, is the ADC Theatre on Park Street, for which ticket bookings can be made at the Arts Cinema box office. Aside from being the central venue for student theatre, the ADC also runs film seasons, especially during the examination period in the middle of Easter Term. The Arts Theatre, on Peas Hill (just off Market Square) is undergoing renovation work at present and handles mostly external touring companies. Its repertoire is varied, and also encompasses opera, dance and musicals. The box office is open from 10am Mon - Sat. The Playroom in St Edward's Passage is also popular for student drama, tickets being available on the door. The Cambridge Drama Centre, off Mill Road, also offers a wide range of plays as well as learning and experimental workshops, with tickets available on the door, and the Junction, off Clifton Road, also stages dance and theatre.

A dance show at the Arts Theatre

Film

Cambridge has two cinemas, the MGM on St Andrew's Street, and the Arts Cinema in Market Passage. The MGM has two screens and shows films on general release, the programme changing every Friday. It also screens late shows, so there are usually up to four films to choose from though there is no advance booking. The Arts Cinema caters for the enthusiast, with continental and the less 'mainstream' films shown every week. During the summer it hosts the Cambridge Film Festival. Its monthly programme is available from the box office or from the Tourist Information Centre in Wheeler Street. Tickets can be purchased in advance from the box office. The ADC Theatre also shows films occasionally (see above).

Music

The musical repertoire of Cambridge is wide and varied. For the Jazz enthusiast the Anchor Pub on Silver Street has a Jazz night on Tuesdays, the Bun Shop on King Street has occasional Jazz nights and the Junction has a Modern Jazz Club. The Old Orleans restaurant on Mill Lane also features Jazz on occasion, as does Flambards Wine Bar, in Rose Crescent, and the Dôme on Bridge Street. The Junction also has gig nights, and The Boat Race pub, on Burleigh Street in the Grafton Centre has a rather heavier selection of bands seven nights a week.

For the classically inclined, the University Music Society performs orchestral and choral works regularly at the University's West Road Concert Hall. The best way to find out what is being performed by college-based orchestral groups is to ask at Porters' Lodges. The most well-known event in this sphere is the choir of King's College, which can be heard during services in the Chapel. Contact the Porters' Lodge at King's for details on 350411. The most all-round venue for music in Cambridge is the Corn Exchange in Wheeler Street, which has in the past attracted artists from the Bolshoi Ballet to the Manic Street Preachers. Tickets are best booked in advance from the box office.

Acting in the recent production of Lorca's Blood Wedding, *at the ADC*

Night Clubs

For those who can do without a night's sleep, there are two night-clubs in the centre of town. Route 66 on Wheeler Street offers a variety of different styles of music depending on which night you choose. More conventional is Cinderella Rockerfellas in Lion Yard, open every night until 2am. The Junction also holds specialised discos which are advertised in its monthly programme. Tickets can be purchased in advance from the Junction box office. The Corn Exchange, on Wheeler Street, also has occasional all-night dance events. Contact the box office for details.

Summer Entertainments

Cambridge City Council traditionally organised the Cambridge Festival in July, but that has now been replaced by a whole summer of events entitled 'Summer in the City', featuring everything from street theatre to drive-in movies and ice skating. Contact the City Council Leisure Department for information.

July's other annual events remain however, including the Fringe, a theatre festival organised by the ADC Theatre, the Film Festival, hosted by the Arts Cinema, and the Folk Festival, traditionally held in the grounds of Cherry Hinton Hall. Contact the Tourist Information Centre or the relevant venues for more details.

Addresses

MGM Cinema, 37, St Andrew's Street
Tel (0223) 64537
Arts Cinema, Market Passage
Tel (0223) 352001
Cambridge Arts Theatre, Peas Hill
Contact Arts Cinema Box Office
ADC Theatre, Park Street
Advance booking from Arts Box Office
Cambridge Drama Centre, Covent Garden, off Mill Road
Tel (0223) 322748
Music Faculty Concert Hall, 11, West Road
Tel (0223) 335185
Flambards Wine Bar, 4 Rose Crescent
Tel (0223) 358108
Dome, 24-26 Bridge Street
Tel (0223) 64961
The Boat Race, Burleigh Street
Tel (0223) 60873
The Corn Exchange, Wheeler Street
Tel (0223) 35781
Route 66, 1 Wheeler Street
Tel (0223) 357503
Cinderella Rockerfellas, Heidelberg Gardens, Lion Yard
Tel (0223) 64222
The Junction, Clifton Road,
off Cherry Hinton Road
Tel (0223) 412600
City Council Leisure Department
Tel (0223) 463363

Taking a bow—a student performer at a recent charity benefit

Shopping

The National Trust shop

The most interesting shops in Cambridge are clustered in the historic city centre, within the ring of the older colleges. With shops selling everything from books to blazers and gifts to gowns, no visitors should have any problems finding suitable souvenirs of their stay in Cambridge.

Edible purchases are easily available. **The National Trust Shop**, on King's Parade, sells a variety of biscuits and jams, and **Bellina**, on All Saints' Passage, sells a mouthwatering array of chocolates. **Fitzbillies**, in Trumpington Street, even post their famous Chelsea Buns worldwide.

There is no shortage of novelty gift shops in the town. The aptly-named **Choice**, in Rose Crescent, is home to a bewildering plethora of gifts which even include chessmen in the shape of Cambridge scholars and fellows. Alternatively, gift ideas are in plentiful supply at **The Friar's House** (Free School Lane). For the wealthier shopper there are a number of imaginative jewellers, including **Catherine Jones** on Bridge St. Also on Bridge St is **Albin Edwards**, which deals in ornamental silver and pewter-ware. For amazing handmade paper-sculpture cards, animal mobiles, and crafts and toys of numerous other kinds, you can't do better than **Balloon** in Fair St, on the way to the Grafton Centre.

For the bored executive, **Chaps** in Green St is a must: a wealth of executive toys guaranteed to keep even the most active mind amused for hours lurks within the door. Just next door is **Past Times**, which sells everything from tapestries to board games, all with an historical theme. More gifts, including fine bed-linen, are on offer in **Perfect Setting**, in All Saints' Passage. And for that extra-cuddly present, a visit to **The English Teddy Bear Shop** on King's Parade, is a must: this cosy shop specialises in teddy bears of all shapes and sizes, every one of them crying out to be taken home!

As you might expect from a university town, Cambridge has more than its fair share of bookshops. Most famous of all is **Heffers**, the official University booksellers, which has customers throughout the world. Their main bookshop is on Trinity Street, as is their children's branch. Other more specialist branches are dotted around the city centre. The **Cambridge University Press**, the oldest university press in the world, also has a shop opposite the Senate House.

Antiquarian booksellers **Deighton Bell**, also in Trinity St, will search for out-of-print volumes on request. Other second-hand bookshops include the two branches of **G David**, one specializing solely in antiquarian books, which can be found in St Edward's Passage, as can the intriguingly-named **Haunted Bookshop**. If these fail you, try **The Bookshop** in Magdalene St, and **The Green Street Bookshop**, which is (surprisingly) in Green St, as are the rare books branch of **Galloway and Porter**, and **Brian Jordan** for music books. On the other hand, if you're after a currently published book, there are a

heffers:

Heffers: Academic & General Bookshop
20 Trinity Street (Tel. 358351)
Over two hundred thousand books in stock, a database of 1¼ million titles, the very latest in computer technology and regular author events. Accounts opened at this shop.

Heffers: Sound, 19 Trinity Street (Tel. 358351)
Classical, jazz, folk and world music on CD and cassette, spoken word recordings and opera and ballet on video. Audio Club discounts available.

Heffers: Art & Architecture, 13 Trinity Street (Tel. 353939)
Books on art and architecture and a selection of postcards and greetings cards.

Heffers: Deighton, Bell, 13 Trinity Street (Tel. 353939)
Secondhand and antiquarian books and prints, plus new titles on bibliography and librarianship. Free search service available for out of print titles.

Heffers: Children's Bookshop, 30 Trinity Street (Tel. 356200)
Offers one of the best selections of books in the country. Also stocks spoken word recordings and videos for children.

Heffers: Paperbacks + Video, 31 St Andrew's Street (Tel. 354778)
A vast selection of paperbacks and videos for sale or rent. Also stocks books on English language learning.

Heffers: Grafton Centre Bookshop (Tel. 313117)
A wide range of general books, children's books, spoken word cassettes and videos.

Open 9am to 5.30pm Monday to Saturday (Paperbacks + Video 6.30pm)

The Cambridge Booksellers

Dillons, Sidney Street

selection of very good high street bookshops, including **Waterstone'** (Bridge Street) and **Dillons** (Sidney Street).

King's Parade is home to two shops which are linked particularly closely to the University. At one end stands the University Outfitters, **Ede and Ravenscroft**, which was founded in 1689. Its windows display the ceremonial gowns it supplies to the dignitaries of the University. At the other end, opposite Great St Mary's Church, is gentlemen's outfitters **Ryder and Amies**, whose windows have been home to many University sports clubs' notice-boards for decades. **A E Clothier**, halfway between the two, also sells scarves, blazers, sports strips and umbrellas in college colours.

For ladies' clothes, the two branches of **Troon**, on King's Parade and nearby in Trumpington St, sell a selective range of designer-label garments. **Hero**, on Green Street, also sells designer clothing. Other fashion shops can be found in Trinity St, Rose Crescent and Bene't Street. Just at the end of Bene't Street, in Peas Hill, is **Raw**, which sells a wide selection of often weird and wonderful 'Doctor Marten' boots. **Greensleeves**, in All Saint's Passage, specialises in clothes made from 100% natural materials, using non-toxic dyes.

Every day except Sunday Cambridge's **Market** provides an alternative way to shop. Stalls selling anything from fresh fruit to old books and from secondhand clothes to wet fish are open most days. On Saturdays, a **Craft Fair** takes place in All Saints' Passage (opposite St John's College), and other art and craft events take place quite often in the Guildhall and Fisher Hall, both situated next to the market.

For the antique and curiosity hunter, King St is particularly rich in interesting shops. Of particular note is the bizarrely—but self-explanatorily—named **My Aunty Had One But She Threw It Away**. Antique dealers **Peter Crabbe** and **Pembroke Antiques** are both on Pembroke Street. Trumpington Street is home to the **Bramwell and Stock** gift shop and **Gabor Cossa Antiques**. Meanwhile, on Bridge St you can find **The Toy Soldier**. Alternatively, if kilims and Afghan clothing are to your taste, **Nomads** in King's Parade is ideal: its wares are mainly from Central Asia and there are many fascinating items to browse over.

Oriental food enthusiasts can buy authentic ingredients and genuine equipment at the **Oriental Stores** on Newnham Rd (next to Sala Thong). Mill Road also boasts several Asian supermarkets.

If you are looking for serious art, **The Gallery on the Cam**, housed in an ingeniously converted river-boat near Jesus Lock (access from Chesterton Road) is a must. Similarly, **Sebastian Pearson**, in Free School Lane, and the **CCA Gallery** in Trinity St deal in fine art and rare prints.

Finally, for those all-important postcards, try **The Postcard Shop** on Bridge Street. If their truly massive selection doesn't satisfy you, **The Lawson Gallery**, in King's Parade, has a wide range of cards and prints, as does the **Fitzwilliam Museum Shop** on Trumpington Street.

Buying flowers in the Market

Restaurants

*All but one of our restaurant reviews were carried out anonymously. Stars are ou
of five (excellent) to one (awful). The symbols in the margin denote the following—*

V—*vegetarian food*	**P**—*piped music*
v—*vegan food*	**S**—*non-smoking area available*
D—*disabled access good*	**O**—*eating outside is possible in*
C—*good facilities for children*	*fine weather*
L—*licensed*	**B**—*booking advisable*
T—*takeaway service*	*The price is for an average three*
M—*live music some nights*	*course meal for two with house wine*

THE TOP DOZEN *(in descending order of price)*

Le Jardin, *Garden House Hotel, Granta Place, Mill Lane*
Tel (0223) 63421. Open all week, for all meals

**V v D C L
M P S O B
£50**

Le Jardin provides you with all that might be expected from a four
star hotel restaurant, at a reasonable price. The set menu dinner, a
£21.50 a head (with some options, a little more), was excellen
value; we enjoyed duck, turbot, lamb and a baked alaska amongst others
Service was excellent; attentive and friendly, but not over-sycophantic
The restaurant's atmosphere is definitely luxurious, with comfortable seat
ing, linen napkins, and silver tableware, but not exclusive; we felt wel
come, relaxed and comfortable, despite the fact that we were not choosing
from the expensive, but probably excellent, à la carte menu. The range o
food served by Le Jardin is extensive, from Chinese to French, and the se
menus, for lunch and dinner change weekly. Sunday roast lunch and
breakfast are also served. A very good place for a special occasion, or an
indulgent dinner.
****

Panos Restaurant, *154-6 Hills Road*
*Tel (0223) 212958/242940. Open all week 12-2.30pm, 7-10.30pm except for
lunch on Sat and Sun*

**V L P B
£50**

This small restaurant, run by Panos Antoniou and his wife
Genevieve, has an intriguing menu with both Greek and French
influences. Start with the mezze for Greek variety, or the casso
lette d'escargots for an excellent variation: deshelled snails in a rich wine
and cream sauce. The ten or so main courses concentrate on steaks and
fish (including salmon and swordfish). We tried and can recommend
Kleftikon (lamb cutlets) and Paleometokhon lamb (lamb steaks in Grand
Marnier). Desserts include horribly sinful crêpe Suzettes (swimming in
honey) and paklavas. The restaurant interior is divided into two intimate
rooms of five tables each, most of which are in alcoves. The service, from
the minute one steps into the conservatory entrance, is exemplary. The
wine list is comprehensive and thoughtfully selected. Set menus are avail
able for £16.50, and set lunches are about £12.
****

V v D C L
T M P O S B
£44

Holiday Inn, *Downing Street*
Tel (0223) 464466. Open all week, for all meals

The atmosphere here is friendly, without being over familiar, the service unhurried and efficient. The surroundings are relaxed and quiet with a varied layout of tables catering for groups of all sizes.

National menus are put on as promotional offers, but English food is always available on request. Our evening was an Italian promotion. The frascati was light and well cooled, the food well presented and appetizing and the selection of vegetables colourful, hot and especially good.

Just the place for parents, but students or those on a budget should not be deterred by the rather formal entrance. Sunday is particularly attractive at £13.95 for a 3 course meal, including half-bottle of wine and a dip in the pool beforehand. Bar snacks are good value and available at lunchtime and in the evening.
****

V v (let them know
beforehand) D C L
O S B
£40

The Old Fire Engine House, *St Mary's Street, Ely*
Tel (0353) 662582. Open for coffee, lunch, tea and dinner save Sunday nights

If you ever need to be convinced that English food can be worthwhile, go to The Old Fire Engine House. The food is interesting, tasty, plentiful, and served with care and generosity. When you have finished your lemon sole in a cream sauce, it is no problem if you want more; all second helpings of main courses are free. Set close to Ely Cathedral, the restaurant proclaims itself with little more than a discreet plaque on the door. When you go in, it is almost as if you are entering somebody's home. The menu varies according to who is cooking that night, contemporary art of all kinds is displayed on the walls and an elegant sitting room is provided for after-dinner coffee and mints. The restaurant doubles as a gallery, with a dedicated room upstairs; exhibitions change monthly, and all work displayed is for sale.
*****

V v D L T B
£40

The Peking Restaurant, *21 Burleigh Street, Grafton Centre*
Tel (0223) 354755. Open 12-2.30pm and 6-11pm

The Peking is in 'real' Cambridge, in the Grafton Shopping Centre. The premises are small, unfussily appointed and the table arrangement means that few people will be annoyed by passing waitresses. The service was prompt and personal; this included the serving of the many courses in the set meal.

The set meal was huge, and something of a bargain at £16. Neither of the reviewers could finish the meal, which can be ordered by a minimum of two people. Of the courses available à la carte, the mixed hot plate (with melt-in-the-mouth seaweed) and the sweet and sour chicken were excellent, although the meal was too much for two people who hadn't eaten anything else that evening. The house white was a sweet Chinese wine.

The food is authentically Chinese, with all food made to the manager's own recipes. The Peking, despite its plain interior, is a good choice for Chinese cuisine.
***

V v
D (will lift down stairs) C L P S B
£40

King's Pantry, *King's Parade*

Tel (0223) 321551. Open everyday for breakfast, lunch, tea and supper, save for Sunday and Monday evenings

King's Pantry is a restaurant with a difference. Acclaimed by *Vegetarian Living* magazine as one of the best vegetarian restaurants in the country, it provides a welcome alternative to the waist-unfriendly indulgences of other Cambridge eating establishments, even if you are a meat-eater. Situated in a basement underneath King's Parade, it presents a wide and original range of wholefood, cooked and presented with flair (all of the main courses were surrounded by a plethora of tropical fruit). Service is amicable and careful, and our fellow diners were so relaxed that they chatted with us, equally intrigued as ourselves by chocolate soup, one of the items on the pudding menu. The restaurant is happy to deal with anybody's special dietary requirements if telephoned.
****

V v (with notice)
D (telephone) C L P S B
£38

Michel's Brasserie, *21-24 Northampton Street*

Tel (0223) 353110. Open daily 12-2.30pm and 6-11pm

Michel's is a hidden pleasure. Tucked away behind St John's College on Northampton Street, opposite The Town and Gown pub, it is a French brasserie which serves delicious, well-priced food. There is hardly any difference in price or quality between the à la carte or fixed price dinner menus, and our meal was served with charm and care. The vegetables were particularly good, tasting fresh and cooked well, although our meat and fish dishes were also impressive. The atmosphere is relaxed and unpretentious, and the clientele seemed to vary from young tourists to old locals. Decorated with pine floors, prints and plants, the interior is smart without being overtly luxurious. Michel's represents very good value for money, especially considering that they always offer a two-course menu rapide for just over seven pounds. Undoubtedly a place worth discovering.
*****

V (ask) L P B
£35

Restaurant Angeline, *8 Market Passage*

Tel (0223) 60305. Open Mon-Sat, 12-2.30pm and 6-11pm, Sun 12-2.30pm

Tucked away above the Arts cinema, the Restaurant Angeline is one of Cambridge's better kept secrets. In a typically French atmosphere you can relax with drinks from the bar whilst your table is being prepared. The food is traditional, simply presented and quite delicious. A good chance to experiment with French cuisine without leaving the country. A selection of irresistible desserts are brought to your table, all freshly made and worth every calorie. Service is discreet and you never feel as if you are being rushed despite the probable second later booking for your table. Weekday lunches can be had very cheaply and Sunday lunches are also offered.
****

V v D L T P S
£30

Standard Tandoori, 52 Mill Road

Tel (0223) 312702. Open 12-2.30pm, 6pm-midnight including bank holidays

A warm barrage of delicate spices and easy, efficient hospitality envelopes you on entering the Standard Tandoori. There is the usual vast array of traditional curry and tandoori dishes, all individually prepared, spiced and well presented, but it is the house specialities that really separate the Standard from the other Indian restaurants in Cambridge. The selection of fish dishes is especially rare and these include the mouth-watering Timatar fish (cooked in peeled tomatoes, fennel, cumin and cayenne pepper) and Standard fish Nawabi (with special fish from Bangladesh). There is also Shah Chicken Jeera Mosalla (mustard seed, cumin, black salt, coriander and paprika) and this reviewer's favourite - Chicken Jalfrezi (green chillis and fresh ginger). These dishes are a little more expensive, but the exquisite tastes are worth every penny. There are also some unusual vegetable side dishes on offer such as Niramish (finely sliced cabbage and peppers). Together, all these make the Standard an interesting place to eat something more than just a curry. ****

V v D L P S (all) B
£27

Sala Thong, 35-37 Newnham Road

Tel (0223) 323178. Open Tue, Thu, Fri, Sat 11am-3pm, 6.30-10pm
Wed 11am-3pm, 6-10.30pm; Sun 12-3pm, 6-10.30pm

Sala Thong is sophisticated: it is exquisitely decorated in the tradition of Thailand and its peaceful environment is ideal for testing Thai cuisine, either as beginner of connoisseur. The food is not a disappointment. Although the menu is small, it is selective and thoughtful. The set menu changes every night and is versatile, providing a good choice for meat eaters, veggies and vegans alike, but if you do not want any restriction there is always à la carte for extras and main dishes. The atmosphere is very relaxed; the proprietor and his staff are extremely friendly as the number of regulars testifies. Sala Thong welcomes a variety of people and has a 'happy hour' from 6.00-7.00pm on Wednesdays and Sundays, to tempt the economically disadvantaged! For those who have enjoyed the food, you can purchase spices from the Oriental Stores next door. ****

V D L
£25

Pizza Express, 7a Jesus Lane

Tel (0223) 324033. Open 11.30am-12.30am every day

You can hardly tell that 7a Jesus Lane is a restaurant, let alone a branch of Pizza Express, a chain of Italian eating places. Its elegant white neo-classical exterior is misleading; the two rooms inside, one wood-panelled and carpeted, the other more of a conservatory, almost seem too smart to be eating a pizza in. All of the décor, however, makes the experience very pleasant and good value for money. Service is prompt and friendly. The menu does diverge from the standard (and very good) pizzas, although they represent the most popular and economical option. Puddings and starters are also good. An excellent place for a smart meal on a lower budget, a late dinner, or just a good, economical meal out. Always popular with students. ***

Tatties, *26-28 Regent Street*

Tel (0223) 358478. Open Mon-Fri 7.45am-9pm, Sat 10am-9pm

'Here the jacket potato is plucked from its humble roots and transformed into a mouthwatering meal in its own right, crammed full with all sorts of imaginitive fillings'. So waxes the publicity for this relaxed, friendly restaurant, a favourite with students. If you consider what you are paying for, then you realise that the price of your meal is a little steep; if you compare it with any other comparable 'fast food' restaurant, then Tatties is ahead on originality, taste, quantity and healthiness. Potatoes can be filled with anything from ratatouille to garlic prawns, and puddings are delicious, if not original (flapjacks, strawberry tarts, ice cream). Service is from a counter at the back of the restaurant, which can be slow at peak times, as there are often queues; this is, of course, a reflection of Tatties popularity. Newspapers, breakfast and coffee are available in the mornings. Well worth a visit.
****

The Best of the Rest

(in alphabetical order)

Blue Boar, *17 Trinity Street*

Tel (0223) 359590. Open for lunch only

VDCLPS
£20-25

The Blue Boar has a reputation as one of the 'in' spots in Cambridge though many students think of it as just a bar. Indeed food is served only during the day, but it's well worth trying. The restaurant has one of the best locations in Cambridge, practically opposite Trinity College on Trinity Street. Its décor is what might be termed 'colonial'; lots of hanging plants and lazily rotating fans. It is a very spacious, clean and efficient restaurant with great character, where the staff were concerned with how our food tasted and not just with getting it to us quickly, though we never felt that we were being rushed. As much thought has gone into vegetarian options on the menu as for meat-eaters so the latter may well find themselves choosing one of these vegetarian dishes. The wine list too was wide-ranging, and the meal overall was extremely well-priced. ***

Browns, *23 Trumpington Street*

Tel (0223) 461655. Open 11am-11.30pm Mon-Sat. Sun 12-11.30pm

VvDCLMPOS
£25-£30

If others can claim to be the Mozarts, Wagners or Stockhausens of the Cambridge restaurant scene, Browns must be its Vivaldi—rarely inspired, but prolific, consistently entertaining and tremendously reliable. Browns has built its well-deserved reputation on providing good food in generous portions at reasonable prices. First-time visitors should warm up at the bar with one of the wide range of cocktails, before seriously considering one of the stupendous salads, the famous steak, mushroom and Guinness pie, or one of the daily specials. For those who still have room, desserts are small but rich. Browns is the place to go if you are young—or want to feel young. Be warned, though: they do not take bookings (they do not need to) and you will have to wait for a table on the busiest evenings. Don't worry—the wait is worth it—and if you cannot wait, Browns also does one of the best late (11.00am) breakfasts in town. ***

Café Piazza, *93 Regent Street*

Tel (0223) 356666. Open daily

VLTMPB
£20

Café Piazza is Cambridge's newest and liveliest pizza parlour, which also doubles as a café. Quite different from 7a Jesus Lane, it has upbeat, louder piped music, and some live music nights; in the past, these have included an acid jazz band. The restaurant is designed to be fun, and it succeeds in being so, although it is primarily a place for the young or young at heart! The pizzas and calzones are made in front of you in the restaurant, and are some of the best in Cambridge; desserts are also good. Service is efficient and relaxed. Cheap, very cheerful, and tasty. ***

**V v C L P O S
B Fri & Sat
£22**

Hobbs Pavilion, *Park Terrace*

Tel (0223) 67480. Open lunches and evenings, Tue-Sat

Pancakes are the speciality at Hobbs Pavilion, where they can be sampled in any number of sweet and savoury forms. The savoury pancakes arrive folded into squares and can be enjoyed with both vegetarian and meat fillings, including the justly famous combination of Bacon, Eggs and Maple Syrup. The sweet pancakes are more exotic to look at, offering tantalising mixtures of ice-cream and chocolate. A range of starters, including homemade soup and delicious smoked meats, is also available and for those unable to cope with two helpings of pancake there is a selection of alternative desserts (particularly noteworthy is the homemade Honey and Lavender ice-cream). In keeping with the reasonable prices on the menu, the house wine is good value. *******

**V D C L P B
£28**

Pasta Galore, *5 Jordan's Yard*

Tel (0223) 324351

Pasta Galore has the advantage of being in the centre, without having a busy road outside: Jordan's Yard is a precinct tucked behind the Round Church car park. The restaurant's interior is airy yet intimate, with wooden floor and light walls; the tables, many of which are doubles, are candlelit.

The Italian menu was very well-priced, yet of a high standard. The starters were light, well-presented and judiciously seasoned; the dressing of the Peperoni alla Piemontese nicely set off the red pepper. The spaghetti bolognese, with oregano and red wine, was excellent, as was the Tagliatella al Amtriciana. The house elderflower cocktail was delicious. The service was very friendly, and the atmosphere perfect for a quiet tête-a-tête. Recommended. *******

Raj-Belash Tandoori, *36-38 Hills Road*

Tel (0223) 354679. Open 12-2.30pm and 6pm-midnight

The Belash has a reputation as one of the best Indian Restaurants in Cambridge and it certainly lives up to it. Service was attentive and prompt, with the added convenience of a hot plate on our table to keep our food warm through the meal. Choice of wines was limited to mainstream favourites (Niersteiner *et al*), though this was perfectly adequate. The range of food on offer was extremely varied, with Tandoori, Raj and Thali style cuisine available, and you can of course specify just how hot you like your curry. A good all round curry house. *******

V v D L T P B

Other restaurants reviewed

V (v) C L T M P S
B £25-30

Cheshmeh, 108 Regent Street Tel (0223) 301073
Persian cuisine in intimate cellar restaurant. Occasional theme nights and poetry readings ***

V C L M B
£25

Chicago Rock Café, 22 Sidney Street Tel (0223) 324600
Spacious American-style Cheers restaurant with great atmosphere ***

V D L P O S B
£35

Dôme Brasserie, 26 Bridge Street Tel (0223) 64961
Offers the atmosphere, food and drink of a French brasserie ***

V (v) (D) C L T M P
O S B
£25

Don Pasquale, 12 Market Hill Tel (0223) 67063
Centrally-located pizzeria and restaurant providing a good range of Italian food ***

V D C L M P S B
£25

Footlights, Grafton Centre Tel (0223) 323434
The place for big groups, good cocktails, Tex-Mex food ***

V D C L P S
£25

Garfunkels, 22-24 Bridge Street Tel (0223) 311053
Family restaurant with wide range of food and cheap buffet ***

V (v) L M P S B
£35

The Greek Taverna, 14a Trinity Street Tel (0223) 302040
Friendly atmosphere with generous portions of home-cooked food ***

V v D L T P S B
£25

La Margherita, 15 Magdalene Street Tel (0223) 315232
Good value pizza parlour ***

V D C L M P O S B
£30

Old Orleans, 10 Miller's Yard Tel (0223) 322777
Cajun and Southern USA food combined with entertaining ambience ***

V (v) L P B
£26

Vivat Brasserie, 1 King's Parade Tel (0223) 359506
Intimate basement restaurant in heart of city ***

Sandwiches, lunches, and snacks

Peppercorns in Rose Crescent offers a galaxy of pies, filled rolls, samosas and cakes, ideal for a quick lunch. **Fitzbillies**, on Trumpington Street, has an excellent upstairs café which offers interesting and delicious food at lunchtime, as well as its downstairs shop which sells sandwiches, baguettes, hot croissants and pasties, and the best selection of pâtisserie in Cambridge. **Trockel, Ullmann & Freunde**, on Pembroke Street, sell a variety of baguettes, organic drinks and sweet things, and a fascinating and esoteric range of cheeses.

Other good Cambridge cake-shops which also sell sandwiches include **Samuel Smiley's**, on Trumpington Street, **Cornucopia**, at the corner of King's Parade and Bene't Street, and **Nadia's**, opposite St John's College in St John's Street. **Nichols Sandwiches**, on Botolph Lane, sells the cheapest sandwiches in Cambridge.

Packaged sandwiches and salads are also available from **Marks and Spencer** (Market Square branch), who are famous for the quality of their food, and **Sainsbury's** (opposite Sidney Sussex College in Sidney Street).

Tea-shops

Afternoon tea is a uniquely English tradition, now exported worldwide. 'High tea', at a table piled high with sandwiches, scones and cakes, has long been a favourite way to end an afternoon. Cambridge has a plethora of tea-shops, suitable for all tastes.

Auntie's Tea Shop, opposite Great St Mary's Church in St Mary's Passage, offers a full waitress service and a wide range of teas and cakes. It does, however, have a minimum charge and can fill up during the summer. A quieter alternative is **The Cambridge Tearoom** on Wheeler Street, conveniently situated opposite the Tourist Information Office. **King's Pantry**, the excellent vegetarian and vegan restaurant in King's Parade, sells full cream teas for £5.95. **Fitzbillies** also serves tea and cakes, as do **Henry's** in Pembroke Street, and **Browns** on Trumpington Street,

For those prepared to forego the convenience of waitress service, the choice widens. Directly across King's Parade from King's College is **The Copper Kettle**. This is one of the better self-service tea-shops, a popular student haunt, and an excellent place from which to watch the people passing by the windows. Other self-service tea-shops include **Belinda's** in Trinity Street and **Eaden Lilley's** **'Food Hall'** in Green Street.

Best of all the tea places around Cambridge, however, must be **The Orchard Tea Garden** in Grantchester (walk three). Serving a

Browns

SNACKS & TEAS

Snacking…

wide range of teas and cakes, and also light lunches, seating is available not only inside but also outside in the extensive orchard on comfortable deck-chairs. The atmosphere seems to invite the visitor to spend the whole afternoon lounging around, and is reminiscent of the days when Virginia Woolf and Wittgenstein took tea in the same place. Regrettably, the Tea Garden is under threat from property developers, and may not be in Grantchester much longer—if it is still there when you read this, make the most of it while it lasts!

Cafés

Don Pasquale

Cambridge boasts a number of more cosmopolitan places for a coffee, croissant or a chat. Most 'studenty' are **Clowns** in King Street and **Martin's Coffee House** at the end of Trumpington Street. **Clowns**, open until midnight, is run by Italians, and serves an excellent espresso and cappucino, as well as quiches, salads and toasted sandwiches. It is usually crowded during termtime. **Martin's** is a popular refuge for students from the Architecture and History of Art faculties opposite. Other cafés include **Don Pasquale** on Market Square and **Café Carrington** on Market Street. **Trockell, Ulmann and Freunde**, on Pembroke Street, also serve coffees, teas, croissants and cakes.

Many pubs, such as **The Eagle** in Bene't Street and **The Maypole** in Park Street, also serve coffee.

Fast food and takeways

Cambridge has its fair share of the usual fast food outlets. These include **Burger King** (St Andrew's Street), **Pizzaland** (Regent Street), and two **Pizza Huts**, also on St Andrew's Street and Regent Street. **McDonald's** has recently come to Rose Crescent, complete with mock ruins in the centre of the restaurant. For fish-lovers, there is a **Nordsee** seafood restaurant in Sidney Street.

However, there are some fast-food outlets with a great deal more character. Most popular with students, especially late at night, is **The Gardenia** restaurant in Rose Crescent (it is open until 3am). Whilst the usual burgers and pizzas are available, it is predominantly a greek restaurant, serving kebabs and filled pitta breads. All are cooked with imagination and flair, and few students make it through their time at Cambridge without several trips to 'Gardies'.

Other places to grab fast food in the daytime are from the **burger and hot dog stands** on Sidney Street and at the corner of Emmanuel Street and Regent Street. The latter is often particularly good, serving food such as barbecued chicken satay rolls and steak sandwiches.

Pubs

Pubs are almost ten-a-penny in central Cambridge. Most of them are owned by the Greene King and Whitbread breweries, although there are a few independent 'free houses' which stock more varied and individual ranges of beers. The choice below is a biased and exclusive selection of our favourite pubs, based on the experience of living as students in Cambridge.

One of Cambridge's largest pubs, and one that every student knows, is **The Anchor** on Silver Street, opposite Queens' College. Inside, drinkers can enjoy their pints on any of the pub's three levels, the lowest of which is often loud and packed in the evenings. The pub has jazz nights upstairs on Tuesday nights, with a cover charge. Outside, there is a terrace right on the Cam, with space for punts to tie up nearby.

The Mill

Just across the road is **The Mill**, well known for its wide range of well-kept 'real ales' which change weekly, and ferociously strong organic scrumpy. Take a look at the blackboard behind the bar to find out which beers are in. A wide range of fruit wines are also stocked. The Mill is particularly pleasant in the summer, when it is possible to take a drink out onto Sheep's Green, the green space opposite, close to the river. Many students choose this pub to celebrate the end of their exams. If you are drinking outside, remember to ask for a plastic glass. **The Granta**, on Newnham Road, next to the Mill Pond, is a large, modern, split-level pub with terraces overlooking the river.

At the other end of the Backs, near Jesus Green, stands the **Spade and Becket**. This has a modern feel. You can sit in the extensive covered bar, or, in the summer, go outside and watch the punts weaving their way down to the lock. A little further along the river is the **Fort St George**, which until the 17th century stood on an island in the middle of the Cam. It is now firmly attached to the banks, on the edge of Midsummer Common. The food is good, and there are sometimes barbecues outside on the terrace in the summer. **The Boat House**, on Chesterton Road, has plenty of seating outside and in, and it is a good place to watch college boat crews plying up and down the river in termtime.

Away from the river, in the city centre, stands **The Eagle**. An enormous place, it belies its recent refurbishment, as the whole interior has been designed to reflect the long history of the pub. Cambridge was once even more full of inns and hostelries, as it was a major trading centre and inland port, and there was great demand for lodgings, stables, refreshment and entertainment for travellers passing through. The Eagle is one of the few places which retains its courtyard, where coaches would pull in to change horses and pick up passengers. The pub was also a favourite with air pilots in the Second World War, a fact which is reflected in the signatures covering the roof of the aptly-named Air Force Bar. Fighter and bomber pilots from the nearby air-

The Eagle, Bene't Street

fields would go to The Eagle to relax, and signed their names, or that of their squadron, on the ceiling. Whilst The Eagle is sometimes packed, and is more expensive than some of its competitors, it is definitely worth a visit. It is open all day, and serves food.

The Mitre and **The Baron of Beef** stand next door to each other on Bridge Street. Both are regular haunts for students from neighbouring St John's College. The Mitre is mid-sized and quite modern, a popular place to be at lunchtime. The Baron of Beef has a very traditional atmosphere, with a good set of regulars. It boasts a bar which is said to be the longest in Cambridge, and a piano and bar billiards. Just across Magdalene Bridge and right opposite Magdalene College is the **Pickerel Inn**, which serves a good range of food at lunchtimes. This was once the alternative bar for Magdalene, and time was when every other drinker sported a college scarf or blazer. Things have changed, however, and today the pub is a pleasant retreat for town, gown and tourists.

The Maypole, near Jesus Green on Park Street, does an excellent line in cocktails. Mario, the landlord, has won national prizes for his cocktail-shaking. He also serves good food. The pub is well-known amongst students for being popular with the University acting community, as it is very close to the ADC Theatre.

A little out of the centre, on King Street, is **The Bun Shop**, three pubs in one. Downstairs are a wine bar, which features occasional jazz nights, and a 'real ale bar', which serves a huge range of cheap and tasty food, including breakfast. Upstairs is a Spanish Tapas Bar. Further along King Street is **The Horse and Groom**, which serves the largest fried breakfast in Cambridge, and the cosy, traditional **Champion of the Thames**. King Street once had far more than its present handful of pubs, and the traditional name for a 'pub crawl' involving a pint in every one was 'The King Street Run.'

If you are prepared to go a little out of the centre of Cambridge, there are a handful of excellent pubs which merit the walk. The **Free Press** in Prospect Row, behind the Police Station on the far side of Parker's Piece, is a hidden treasure. Quiet, with superbly-kept real ales and log fires and candles in the winter, it also serves good food. Watch out for the rabbits in the backyard garden. Please note that it is a smoke-free pub.

Both **The Clarendon Arms**, in Clarendon Street (again, near Parker's Piece) and the **Panton Arms**, in Panton Street (off Lensfield Road) serve large, economically-priced traditional English Sunday roasts. 'The Clarry' is a particular favourite with students from nearby Emmanuel College. Further afield, **The Live and Let Live**, on the corner of Mawson Road and Cross Street, has a cosy, local atmosphere without being hostile.

For the very adventurous, **The Phoenix** in Histon reputedly has the best Chinese food in Cambridge (book well in advance), and **The Wrestlers** on the Newmarket Road is the place to eat Thai. Both, however, get very crowded, and The Wrestlers' occasional live music is not necessarily to everybody's tastes.

The Free Press

SNACKS & TEAS

Out of town

There is more to Cambridgeshire than just the city of Cambridge. The area round about has a rich cultural heritage, and if you have a few days to spend, you could do worse than escape the bustle of the town centre and range further afield. Here are just a few of the best sights and sites.

Near Cambridge

Closest of all the delightful villages clustered around Cambridge is **Grantchester**. See walk three for more details. Between Grantchester and the neighbouring village of Trumpington lies **Byron's Pool**, a pond where the poet often bathed while an undergraduate at Trinity College.

Three miles west of Cambridge along the A1303 lies the quiet village of **Madingley**. Near the village are the 16th century **Madingley Hall**, where the fleeing Charles I stayed, and England's only **American Military Cemetery**. Open daily, the cemetery's hauntingly landscaped grounds provide the resting place for 3,811 American servicemen who died while operating from British bases during World War II, and its Memorial Wall carries the names of 5,215 servicemen whose graves are unknown.

Ancient earthworks can be found on Cambridge's **Gog Magog Hills** (two miles south of the city along the A1307). Wandlebury Ring is the remains of a first-century Iron-Age hill fort. The building in its centre is the stable block of a 18th century mansion; it covers the grave of the horse Godolphin Arab, forebear of many English racehorses, who was buried there in 1753.

Just on the edge of the tiny village of Lode, five miles north-east of Cambridge along the B1102, stands **Anglesey Abbey**, a beautiful mansion built in the 1590s on the site of a 12th century Augustinian priory. Owners have included Sir George Downing, founder of Downing College in Cambridge, and Lord Fairhaven, whose art collections are displayed throughout the house, and who created the spectacular 100-acre Georgian-style grounds.

Chapel, American Cemetery

Further afield

Jungle Book fans should be prepared for the 25-minute drive to the former home of Kipling's daughter, **Wimpole Hall** (nine miles to the south-west along the A603). Started in 1640, the house was completed in the 18th century, and the grounds were landscaped by Capability Brown in 1770. The landscaping involved the complete demolition of the original village of Wimpole and its rehousing at New Wimpole, along the main road.

Nearer Cambridge at Duxford Airfield (8 miles south of Cambridge, off Junction 10 on the M11) is the **Imperial War Museum**. Lurking in the hangars are more than 100 aircraft, ranging from crude bi-planes to the prototype Concorde. For the intrepid, flights around the airfield are sometimes on offer, and there's always the consolation of the flight simulator for those who want to do the driving. The museum also has exhibitions featuring midget submarines and other fascinating details of military developments over the last hundred years.

For those who prefer leopards to weaponry, a visit to **Linton Zoo** is a must. Ten miles south-east of Cambridge along the A1307, the ten-acre family-run Zoo houses bears, owls, Iynxes, the rare Indian eagle owl and the binturong (a long-haired Asian mammal), all in well-maintained grounds.

Anglesey Abbey

Far out

A little further afield (fifteen miles south along the A130) is the beautiful mediaeval town of **Saffron Walden**. Its name is taken from the Saffron crocus, grown here for its orange dye until late last century, and which appears on the town's coat of arms. The town also benefited greatly from the wool trade, and its imposing church bears witness to its wealth and prosperity during mediaeval times. The town's many surviving 16th century houses boast striking displays of 'pargetting' (ornamental plasterwork), especially in Church St. One mile west of Saffron Walden stands the magnificent 17th century Jacobean **Audley End House**. Originally three times its present size, it was dubbed by James I as "too large for a king". The interiors have benefited from the talents of Sir John Vanbrugh and Robert Adam, while the gardens were landscaped by Capability Brown. Rides are often available on a miniature railway which runs round the grounds.

Fifteen miles east of Cambridge along the A45 and A11 lies the county's horseracing Mecca, **Newmarket**. Races have been held at the town since the first gold cup race in 1635, and the full story can be had at the **National Horse-Racing Museum** in the High St. For the less horsey there is the seven-mile Devil's Dyke, a 6th century earthwork built to defend the Saxon inhabitants from hostile tribes to the south.

Ely (16 miles north-east along the A10) is best known for its spectacular 12th and 14th century Cathedral. Its remarkable octagonal tower can be seen for miles across the Fens, and seeing it gives sense to the old name 'the Isle of Ely', which dates from the time when the town was on an island in the Fens. The town was once home to Oliver Cromwell, and more can be discovered at the **Ely Museum**, just north of the Cathedral.

Huntingdon (16 miles north-west along the A604) was once the county town of the now abolished Huntingdonshire. It was also the birthplace of Oliver Cromwell, and the Cromwell Museum provides a record of his life. It is housed in a former grammar school at which both Cromwell and the diarist Samuel Pepys were pupils, each in his day. Not far to the west of Huntingdon stands **Hinchingbrooke House**, a 16th century mansion which was once home to a branch of the Cromwell family. Built on the site of a defunct Augustinian nunnery, it is now a school, but is often open to visitors, with senior pupils acting as guides.

Details

Please note that all details are subject to change.
Details given are correct as of July 1993.

ANGLESEY ABBEY
Tel. (0223) 811200
House: 27 March-17 October: *Open Wed-Sat 1.30-5.30pm, Sundays*
and Bank Holiday Mondays 1-5.20pm
12 July-7 September: *also open Sundays 11am-5.20pm. Last*
admission: 5pm
Garden: 27 March-11 July: *Open Wed-Sun 11am-5.30pm*
(last admission 5pm)
Closed Good Friday
Admission charge: £4.50 House and grounds
£2.50 grounds only. Sundays £5.50/£3
National Trust Members free
Disabled access good, but 24 hours' notice appreciated

AUDLEY END HOUSE
Tel. (0799) 522399 or 522842
House open Easter to October Wed-Sun and Bank Holiday Mondays 1-5pm
Grounds open 12-5pm. Admission £4.90/£3.70/£2.40

CROMWELL MUSEUM
Tel. (0480) 425830
1 April-31 Oct: Open Tue-Fri 11am-1pm and 2-5pm, Sun 2-4pm
1 Nov-31 Mar: Open Tue-Fri 1-4pm, Sat 11am-1pm and 2-4pm, Sun 2-4pm
Admission free
Entrance has two steps. Museum is on ground floor only

Duxford

DUXFORD IMPERIAL WAR MUSEUM
Tel. (0223) 835000
Open: March to October 10am-6pm (last admission 4.45pm or dusk)
Rest of year 10am-4pm
Closed 24-26 Dec, 1 Jan
Telephone for occasional flying days
Disabled access; no advance warning needed

ELY CATHEDRAL
Tel. (0353) 667735
Open Winter months 7.30am-6pm (Sun 7.30am-5pm)
Summer months 7am-7pm
Admission £2.60/£2.10
Ramps all around cathedral

HINCHINGBROOKE HOUSE
Tel. (0480) 451121
Open May to August, Sun and Bank Holiday Mondays 1-5pm
Not open during week
Admission £1.50/£1
Flights of stairs (no lift)

LINTON ZOO
Tel. (0223) 891308
Open every day (except Christmas Day) 10am-6pm (or dusk)
Last admission 5.15pm
Admission £3.50/£2.50/£3
No stairs; disabled toilets

**The Cemetery,
Madingley**

AMERICAN MILITARY CEMETERY, MADINGLEY
Tel. (0954) 210350
Open mid-April to September 8am-6pm
    October to mid-April 8am-5pm
Gates close 30 minutes before closing time
Admission free
Steps in chapel may be a problem, otherwise completely accessible to those in wheelchairs

NATIONAL HORSE RACING MUSEUM
Tel. Newmarket (0638) 667333
Open late March to early December;
    Tuesday to Saturday and Bank Holidays 10am-5pm
    Sundays 2-5pm (last admission 4.30pm)
Also open Mondays in July and August
Admission £2.50/£1.50
Completely accessible to wheelchair-bound

WIMPOLE HALL
Tel. (0223) 207257
Open March to October, Tue-Thu, Sat and Sun 1-5pm
Park open sunrise to sunset
Home Farm open 10.30am-5pm
Admission charge: Hall and Farm £6/£3; Hall only £4.50/£2; Farm only £3.50/£1.50. National Trust members: Hall is free; Farm half-price
Disabled access – contact office

Churches

Cambridge has many picturesque and ancient churches which are well worth visiting. A few are as old as the city itself, and many are remarkably beautiful.

ST BENE'T'S CHURCH (ST BENEDICT'S)
Bene't Street
St Bene't's Saxon tower is the oldest building in Cambridge. It was probably built around 1025, while the nave was rebuilt in the 13th century. Other parts were added in the 14th and 15th centuries, including the gallery connecting the church with neighbouring Corpus Christi College. St Bene't's served as Corpus' chapel for over 300 years.

ST EDWARD, KING AND MARTYR
St Edward's Passage
This church, tucked away behind King's Parade, is dedicated to the Saxon king, Edward the Confessor. Most of the building dates from the 15th century, although the tower is probably 12th century. The aisles were built around 1450 by Trinity Hall and Clare Hall, to serve as college chapels after their local church was pulled down to make way for King's College.

GREAT ST MARY'S, THE UNIVERSITY CHURCH
King's Parade
The present church was built in 1478 to replace an earlier 14th century one. Formerly known as 'St Mary's by the Market', it is still used for some University ceremonies, and the University sermon is preached there every Sunday evening during term. The church is also the starting-point from which the first milestones in Britain were measured: undergraduates are still required to live within three miles of it in order to count 'in residence'. The tower of the church, which was built in 1608, is usually open to the public, and provides panoramic views over the city.

LITTLE ST MARY'S CHURCH
Trumpington Street
The church was originally dedicated to St Peter, and acted as chapel for Peterhouse until 1632. It was rebuilt and re-dedicated to the Virgin Mary in 1350. Near the entrance is a memorial to Godfrey Washington, who died in 1729, a fellow of Peterhouse and relative of George Washington. The memorial includes the Washington crest of three stars and stripes surmounted by an eagle, which was the basis for the flag of the United States of America.

THE ROUND CHURCH (HOLY SEPULCHRE CHURCH)
Round Church Street
This is one of the very few churches in Britain built with a circular nave to commemorate the Holy Sepulchre in Jerusalem. Erected in 1130, the chancel and north aisle were rebuilt in the 15th century. The present roof is a 19th century replacement for the original 15th century polygonal bell-tower, which was removed during the course of restoration work carried out by Anthony Salvin in 1841.

Bene't Street church

Punting

Punts by Trinity

There is no better way to see the Backs on a summer's day than from the cool embrace of a punt. Punting is the quintessence of the Cantabrigian myth—a handsome young man wearing boater and blazer guiding his craft below the eight bridges, with a beautiful woman smiling up at him as he glides down the Cam. The picture almost holds true today, although blazer and boater have given way to T-shirt and baseball cap—punting still remains one of the favourite ways for the Cambridge undergraduate to relax.

While most colleges don't hire their punts out to the public, it is possible for the visitor to hire a punt for the day or by the hour, with or without the services of an experienced punt-chauffeur, from one of the punt-hire companies operating along the river.

Punt-chauffeur services may offer anything from a full day's outing, complete with packed hamper and expert commentary on the sights, to little more than a competent hand on the pole. The more adventurous or athletic, however, may hire a punt by the hour from any of the jetties along the river, and do the driving for themselves.

Tips for punters

Before you start, there are one or two preparations you can make. Don't wear clothing that could be stained by river water. While punts are extremely difficult to capsize, it is very easy to fall out of one, especially if you are standing up. In addition, when handling the pole, water tends to run down your arm, so it is best to roll up your sleeves. Do wear shoes with good grips—if you have smooth soles, bare feet are probably a better bet.

Always stand squarely on the platform at the rear of the punt. If you feel insecure there, you can stand in the well behind the seats, thought this makes the punt harder to control. Try not to stand towards one side of the punt, as this will make it lean alarmingly.

The main problems that newcomers to punting face tend to centre around using the pole correctly. Hold the pole vertical directly at your side, with the end just above the water. Let it slip fast through your fingers, so that it hits the river bed. Holding with both hands, push downwards on the pole so that it tilts forwards. Make sure that the pole moves parallel to the punt—if it tilts at an angle, the punt will move to the side and swing round. If this happens, don't panic. Hold the pole so that it drags in the water behind the punt. Holding it at a shallow angle, half way out of the water, with your bottom hand quite low down the pole, use the pole as a rudder. If you point the pole to the left, the punt will move to the left, and vice versa. Once you're on course, pull the pole up and let it down as before, repeating the stroke to build up speed.

Moored punts

When you're on the move, beware of a few notorious pitfalls:

• Don't attempt to get in a stroke before a bridge unless there are at least two full lengths of a punt in front of you. Poles are long things, and when they get jammed between the arch of a bridge and a river bed, you're in for trouble.

• Don't be tempted to hold onto the pole if it gets stuck in the river bed or against a bridge. Poles float, and can be retrieved by paddling back. If you hold on, the punt will drift onwards and you will slide off, clutching the pole. If you feel the pole sticking, twist it as you pull, but if it stays stuck, let it go!

• Beware of the deep areas under Magdalene Bridge (it's the big cast-iron road bridge next to Magdalene and St John's colleges). The river there is deeper than the length of some poles, so hang onto yours and just drift through.

• If you do fall in, don't drink the water. If you swallow any, seek medical advice, and be careful not to contaminate any cuts with river-water.

Where to go

There are two classic punting routes in Cambridge. The first is from Magdalene Bridge to Silver Street Bridge. This lasts about an hour, and takes you along the famous backs of the colleges, beneath all the bridges in the city centre. Especially beautiful is the stretch between St John's Bridge of Sighs and Queens' Mathematical Bridge.

The other route is up-river from Silver Street to the delightful village of Grantchester. This lasts an afternoon and takes you through Grantchester Meadows, made famous by Rupert Brooke; you can moor at a bank there and picnic in pleasant surroundings, or buy a drink at one of the nearby pubs.

Punt companies

All punt companies require a deposit on hire punts. Chauffeur punt trips vary in length, between 40 minutes and an hour for going along the Backs, and are longer (and dearer) for going up river towards Grantchester. All telephone numbers have the Cambridge (0223) prefix if you are ringing from outside the area, and all prices are subject to change.

BLUE RIVER PUNT COMPANY
By the Spade and Becket pub, Jesus Green
Tel: 60569
Open: 10am - 5pm and most evenings
Weekly rate, per hour: £6
Weekend rate, per hour: £8
Deposit: £30
Chauffeur Punt: from £12-£30

PUNTING

Jolly boating weather…

**Watching from
the banks**

CAMBRIDGE PUNT COMPANY
Anchor Pub
Tel: 357565
Open: 10am - 9pm
Weekly rate, per hour: £7
Weekend rate, per hour: £8
Deposit: £40
Chauffeur Punt: from £15

GRANTA PUNT COMPANY
Granta Pub, Newnham Road
Tel: 301845
Open: 10am - dusk
Weekly rate, per hour: £5
Weekend rate, per hour: £6
Deposit: £30
Chauffeur Punt: from £12

SCUDAMORES
Quayside (by Magdalene Bridge) and two at Mill Lane (by the Mill pub)
Punts from Quayside are only available for use on the Backs. Chauffered
punts, guided tours and picnics can be arranged.
Tel: 359750 (hire punts), 321697 (chauffeur punts)
Open: 10am - 6pm
Weekly rate, per hour: £7
Weekend rate, per hour: £8
Deposit: £30
Chauffeur Punt: from £15

TRINITY COLLEGE PUNT HIRE
Garret Hostel Lane
Tel: 338483
Open 10am - 5.45pm, punts back by 6.45pm
Weekly rate, per hour: £7
Weekend rate, per hour: £8
Deposit: £30
Chauffeur Punt: from £15

TYRRELLS MARINE
Quayside
Trips are negotiable for big parties
Tel: 63080
Open: 10am - dusk
Weekly and weekend rate: £4.80 for first hour plus £1.20 per quarter hour
afterwards
Deposit: £25
Chauffeur Punt: from £15

Hotels

The Holiday Inn, Downing Street

Accommodation in Cambridge is usually difficult to find during the peak summer season, especially during 'May Week', (mid-June), around Graduation Day (late June/early July) and during the Cambridge festivals (late July). As a rule, it is wise to book well in advance.

This is by no means an exhaustive list of Cambridge's hotels, and inclusion does not imply our recommendation. More details of this and other types of accommodation, such as the YHA and YMCA, are available from the Tourist Information Office on Wheeler Street, which will also make reservations for you.

Prices are intended only as a guide. Most hotels include the price of a full English breakfast in the room price.

ARUNDEL HOUSE HOTEL
53 Chesterton Road, CB4 3AN Tel (0223) 67701
Single £37.50-£53.50, Double £53.50-£72.50

CAMBRIDGE LODGE HOTEL
139 Huntingdon Road, CB3 0DQ Tel (0223) 352833
Single £60, double £65

GARDEN HOUSE HOTEL
Granta Place, CB2 1RT Tel (0223) 63421
Single £86, double £120

GONVILLE HOTEL (BEST WESTERN)
Gonville Place, CB1 1LY. Tel (0223) 66611
Single £65, Double £82

HAMILTON HOTEL
156 Chesterton Road, CB4 1DA Tel (0223) 65664
Single £20-£30, double £30-£45

HOLIDAY INN
Downing Street, CB2 3DT Tel (0223) 464466
Single £53-£95, double £106

REGENT HOTEL
41 Regent Street, CB2 1AB Tel (0223) 351470
Single £52.50, double £69.50

ROYAL CAMBRIDGE HOTEL
Trumpington Street, CB2 1PY Tel (0223) 351631
Single £69.50, double £79.50

UNIVERSITY ARMS HOTEL
Regent Street, CB2 1AD Tel (0223) 351241, Fax (0223) 31526
Single £81-86, Double £110-115

Useful information

The Cambridge Tourist Information Office

Tourist information

CAMBRIDGE
Tourist Information Centre, Wheeler Street
Tel (0223) 322640
Gives details of tours, including private group tours, as well as a multitude of useful information for the tourist. Please note that any group o ten or more persons wishing to visit the colleges must be accompanie by a blue badge Cambridge guide.
Note—King's, St John's, Queens' and Clare Colleges charge all tourists fo entrance.

Other Towns
ELY: Oliver Cromwell House, 29, St Mary's Street
        Tel (0353) 662062
HUNTINGDON: c/o Library, Princes Street
        Tel (0480) 425831
SAFFRON WALDEN: 1 Market Place, Market Square
        Tel (0799) 524282
PETERBOROUGH: 45, Bridge Street
        Tel 0733 317336

Travel

Travel Agents
American Express Travel Service, 25 Sidney Street Tel (0223) 324432
Campus Travel, 5 Emmanuel Street Tel (0223) 324283/60201
STA Travel, 38 Sidney Street Tel (0223) 66966
Thomas Cook Travel, 18 Market Hill Tel (0223) 66141/357356/67724

Air
CAMBRIDGE AIRPORT, Newmarket Road
        Tel (0223) 61133
Tours and charter flights: Magnet Air Services, Tel (0223) 293621
Air taxi service: contact Captain Richie at Cecil Aviation
        Tel (0223) 294218

USEFUL INFO

TOURIST INFORMATION TOURS

The Backs ½ mile

Fitzwilliam Museum ⅓ mile

Scott Polar Museum ⅔ mile

Botanic Gardens ¼ mile

Whipple Museum of Science 250 yds

Sedgwick Museum of Geology ⅓ mile

Wondering where to go?

Drummer Street
Bus Station

STANSTED AIRPORT, Stansted
Offers a wide variety of national and international flights
For information telephone (0279) 662379 or (0279) 662520
The airport is approximately 30 minutes' drive from Cambridge, south along the M11

Bus
CAMBRIDGE COACH STATION, Drummer Street
Intercity buses:
       National Express: Tel (0223) 460711
       Cambridge Coach Services: (0223) 236333
Local buses: Cambus, Tel (0223) 423554

Railway
CAMBRIDGE RAILWAY STATION,
Tel (0223) 311999
Talking Timetables:
Cambridge to London (Mon-Fri): (0223) 359602
Cambridge to London (Sat): (0223) 467098
Cambridge to London (Sun): (0223) 353465

Car Hire
Children's car seats can be booked from those marked (c)
AVIS RENT-A-CAR, 245 Mill Road Tel (0223) 212551 (c)
BUDGET RENT-A-CAR, 303-5 Newmarket Road. Tel (0223) 212551
CAMKARS HIRE, 362 Milton Road Tel: (0223) 425706
HERTZ RENT-A-CAR, Barnwell Road Tel (0223) 416634
KENNING CAR HIRE, 47, Coldham's Lane. Tel (0223) 61538 (c)
EURODOLLAR CAR HIRE, 264 Newmarket Road
       Tel (0223) 65438 (c)

Car Parking
Warning: Parking in central Cambridge can be extremely difficult. Do not park illegally (on yellow lines or elsewhere), or there is a risk that your car will be removed without notice. The current fee for removal is £125.
If your car is removed, you will need to retrieve it from Clifton Road off Cherry Hinton Road. Telephone Parkside Police on (0223) 358966 for more details.
Parking restricted to 'pay and display' bays throughout central Cambridge 9 am-5.30pm, Mon-Sat.
CAR PARKS:
Short Stay: Lion Yard, Park Street, Grafton Centre (Maid's Causeway, East Road)
Long Stay: Gonville Place, Saxon Street, Gold Street
Coach Park: City Football Ground, Milton Road

Horse and Carriage Tours
THE CAMBRIDGE HORSE AND CARRIAGE COMPANY
Spade and Becket Pub, Jesus Green Tel (0223) 60569

Students Go for Less

At Campus Travel we specialise in low cost travel for students and under 26's. Call into a branch near you and discover a world of possibilities.

- ■ By Plane, Boat and Train
- ■ Round the World Flights
- ■ Adventure Tours
- ■ Travel Insurance
- ■ Student Travel Cards
- ■ Eurotrain & Inter-Rail

Campus Travel
5 Emmanuel Street
Cambridge CB1 1NE
Tel: 0223 324 283

also at
Campus Travel
YHA Adventure Shop
6-7 Bridge Street
Cambridge CB2 1UA
Tel: 0223 60201

And Branches
Nationwide

Ivy-clad bike

Bicycle Hire
H DRAKE, 56-60 Hills Road, Cambridge   Tel (0223) 634681
GEOFF'S BIKE HIRE, 65 Devonshire Road, Cambridge
            Tel (0223) 65629
MIKE'S BIKES, 28 Mill Road   Tel (0223) 312591

Alternative Cambridge
The following is a list of the shops which are recommended by The Little
Green Book, *the students' guide to being 'green' in Cambridge*:

OXFAM, Bridge Street (clothes, stationery, cosmetics)
BODY SHOP, Lion Yard (cosmetics)
CULPEPER, Lion Yard (cosmetics, herbs, etc.)
NATIONAL TRUST SHOP, King's Parade (gifts, stationery, cosmet-
ics)

Cambridge boasts two other dedicated 'green' shops; ARJUNA
WHOLEFOODS, a co-operative, on Mill Road, and
GREENSLEEVES, in All Saint's Passage, which sells clothes made
with 100% natural materials and non-toxic dyes.

Central recycling points are on Corn Exchange Street and by the car
park on Park Street.

Taxis

Taxi ranks on St Andrew's Street and at Railway Station

Help and advice

Emergency:
Dial 999 and ask for Ambulance, Fire or Police as required (24 hour)

Hospital: Addenbrooke's Hospital, Hills Road
      Tel (0223) 245151

Chemist/ Pharmacist:
Boots, 28 Petty Cury & 65 Sidney Street
Tel (0223) 350213

Coulson Horace and Sons, 66 Bridge Street
Tel (0223) 353002

Lloyds Chemist, 30 Trumpington Street
Tel (0223) 359449

Phone Line Services:
Citizens' Advice Bureau: Tel (0223) 353875
Samaritans: Tel (0223) 64455 (24 hour)
Rape Crisis: Tel (0223) 358314 (24 hour)

Post Offices:
9-11 St Andrew's Street (Main Post Office, last collection Mon-Fri 7.45pm) Tel (0223) 323325
23-24 Trinity Street
2a Trumpington Street

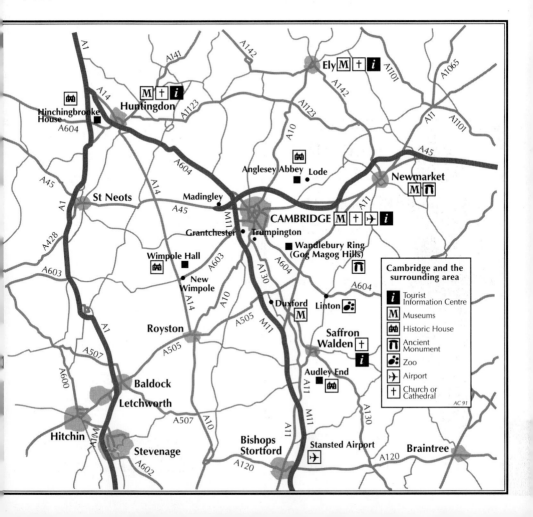

Cambridge and the surrounding area

i Tourist Information Centre
M Museums
🏠 Historic House
🏛 Ancient Monument
🦁 Zoo
✈ Airport
✝ Church or Cathedral

AC 91

Index